D1639572

THE ROUTEMASTER POCKET-BOOK

COMPILED AND INTRODUCED
BY MATTHEW JONES

CONWAY

Acknowledgements

Numerous individuals helped with the compilation of this pocket-book at the research stage and during visits to various museums and archives. Thanks are therefore due to the following in particular for their assistance: Stephanie Rousseau at Transport for London Historical Archives and the accommodating staff at 55 Broadway; Caroline Warhurst, Library & Information Services Manager and Anna Renton, Curator – both of the London Transport Museum; all the staff at British Library Newspapers, Colindale; Gavin Booth of Bus Users UK; Andrew Morgan, Chairman of the Routemaster Association; and transport photographer and journalist John Lidstone. This book is dedicated to A. A. M. Durrant – for without his industry and endeavour the Routemaster would not have existed – and to Heather; for without her support and encouragement this book would not have existed.

First published in 2012 by Conway,
An imprint of Anova Books Ltd
10 Southcombe Street
London W14 0RA
www.conwaypublishing.com

10 9 8 7 6 5 4 3 2 1

A CIP record for this book is available from the British Library.

ISBN 9781844861521

Printed and bound by WS Bookwell, Finland

Publishers' Note.

In this edition, references to material not included in the selected extract have been removed to avoid confusion, unless they are an integral part of a sentence. In these instances the note [not included here] has been added.

CONTENTS

Section. Page

Acknowledgements 2
Introduction 4
1 Learning to be a Bus Driver .12
2 Behind the Scenes 20
3 Timetables and Duty Schedules 27
4 Public Service Vehicle Licences and Regulations 38
5 Loading and Unloading of Buses in Relation to Vehicle Design 44
6 London Transport's New Double-Deck Bus 49
7 West End Sees London's 64-Seater; New London Bus Gives More Room 63
8 London's 'Bus of the Future' Goes Into Service: The Routemaster to be tried out on Route 2 65
9 Comments, Suggestions & Criticisms 73
10 The Use of Routemaster Buses 76
11 Routemasters in Service 93
12 A.E.C. 1000th Routemaster .96
13 London Transport's Thirty-Foot Routemaster Bus: Longer 72-seat Vehicles Go Into Service . . .100
14 Illuminated Advertisements on LT Buses 102
15 LT Routemaster Buses: A Technical Description . . .106
16 Instructions for Drivers and Conductors 119
17 The Gibson Self-Printing Bus Ticket Issuing Machine: A User's Guide .123
Bibliography 128

INTRODUCTION

The A.E.C. Routemaster bus holds a unique place in the history of London Transport and indeed in the history of public service vehicle design. Specifically designed and constructed for service in the tough operating conditions of London and its suburbs, it served this vast area for nearly half a century. Its utility and mechanical reliability made it a dependable workhorse for London Transport (LT), leading to several refurbishments and life extensions. Routemaster buses grew to be as familiar a sight in the capital as the red telephone box or the London black cab.

Such long service bred almost universal affection, and the decision, taken in 2005, to phase out the Routemaster in favour of modern and accessible low-floor types was met with dismay and considerable resistance. Nevertheless its withdrawal went ahead, and the last official running day of the Routemaster in regular service was Friday 9 December 2005. This day, dubbed 'Black Friday' by bus enthusiasts, saw crowds lining the number 159 route (Marble Arch–Streatham), the last remaining Routemaster bus route.

Since then the Routemaster's requiem has been covered in detail, particularly as nostalgia for this venerable vehicle has swelled. Other books have focused on recording Routemasters in photographs or on providing technical details for operation and maintenance of preserved examples. Researchers, enthusiasts and historians are fortunate in that much of the documentation pertaining to the development of the Routemaster has been preserved and archived. There is undoubtedly considerable value in re-examining these original sources and presenting those of relevance in a single volume, and that is the approach that has been taken in this book.

The first extract is drawn from *The Bus Driver*, published in 1961. This was one volume in a series on 'People's Jobs' produced by the Educational Supply Association – a firm better known as manufacturers of classroom furniture.[1] Aimed at prospective school-leavers, the chapters are couched in simple language but nevertheless give a good insight into the training and daily duties of a bus driver, and offer a glimpse 'behind the scenes' at a typical bus garage. The information contained here is wide-ranging and applicable to the industry as a whole rather than specific to LT Routemaster operation, yet it evokes an eminently practical world concerned primarily with the provision of a reliable and regular service for passengers, run according to a strict timetable. Such lessons would have been more than familiar to the men of the Central and Country Area buses, and the Green Line coaches that served London and its environs at this time.

Timetable compilation was an art in itself; a specialised job that, as mentioned in 'Behind the Scenes', was the preserve of the scheduling office. The essential handbook for those tasked with such a job was J. F. Turner's *Timetable and Duty Schedule Compilation (Road Passenger Transport)*, which first appeared in 1946. Turner's introduction helpfully lists a series of terms vital to the busmen, many pertaining to the various aspects of a bus crew's duty as well as to a busman's relief, rest-days and time allowances.

Such entitlements, along with rates of pay, were central concerns for busmen. The industry was strongly unionised, and in 1958 discontent over wage policies led to the famous 'Busman's Strike', led by Frank Cousins, General Secretary of the Transport and General Workers Union.[2] The strike saw the complete withdrawal of all Central and Country area buses from 5th May to 20th June, and Pathé newsreels from this period show deserted bus stands and thousands of commuters thronging London streets as they walked to work.[3] Indeed, the introduction of the Routemaster into service was delayed because of the ongoing dispute. The busmen eventually returned to work on 21st June, but much damage was done – some services that had been cut were never reinstated, while many passengers, forced to find alternative means of transport, purchased cars, motorcycles and scooters, and never returned to the buses.

London Transport had rightly been concerned about the rise of private transport as disposable income among the middle classes increased in the postwar period. Accordingly initial design work for the Routemaster stressed that the main competition for prospective passengers came from the 'private car', and efforts were made to ensure that levels of comfort were of comparable standard. This was part of a much broader appraisal in which the whole concept of the bus as a passenger carrying vehicle was comprehensively re-examined. As A.A.M. Durrant, Chief Mechanical Engineer (Road Services) put it, in a talk delivered to garage and depot staff at Chiswick Works in 1957:

> 'We decided to start from rock bottom and make a complete re-assessment, not only of the engineering aspect of the design but of the operating specification – the operating requirement for the new vehicle … the aim being to get down to the ideal bus.'[4]

Durrant goes on to emphasise the importance of operational research to the design process, and as an example cites the research undertaken to ascertain 'what influence the width of the conductor's platform had upon the speed of loading and unloading of the vehicle', since of course, these are vital factors that affect the average operating speed and thus the efficiency of service. The report that summarised these findings is reproduced. The conclusions drawn were a major factor in the decision to adopt a rear platform for the Routemaster, a feature that was already in use at that time on existing LT buses (such as the RT type), with some modifications – including the integration of a 'cubbyhole' for the conductor to stand in, an innovative feature that aided the flow of boarding and alighting passengers.

The design team was directed by A. A. M. Durrant and Colin Curtis, while industrial designer Douglas Scott was responsible for vehicle styling. Together they successfully evolved a double-decker bus that was particularly suited to cope with city working, with long life and economy in both operation and maintenance. The extensive design work was justified by the assertion that no existing commercial bus design was suitable for London Transport's requirements or for widespread service in the capital.

The bus featured two steel sub frame assemblies coupled to a lightweight aluminium alloy body. This 'integral' method of construction obviated the need for a chassis and enabled considerable savings in weight. Essentially it meant that the body structure itself was the main load-carrying member, with groups of mechanical units mounted on front and rear sub-frames, designated the 'A-frame' and 'B-frame' respectively. In addition, the Routemaster incorporated many advanced features. These included independent front wishbone coil suspension with coil spring suspension at the rear; a continuous flow pressure-hydraulic braking system; power-assisted steering and automatic transmission, controlled through a fluid flywheel and epicyclic gearbox, regulated by electro-pneumatic valves. These were controlled by the accelerator pedal in conjunction with a speed sensitive generator (SSG), and provision was made for automatic operation of second, third and top gears – only first and reverse gears were manually operated, although manual operation could over-ride the automatic system for all gears if required. The clutch pedal was therefore eliminated, enabling two-pedal operation for the driver along with a five-position gear selector lever mounted on the steering column. One much-heralded benefit of the installation was that it produced 'constant drive', i.e. at no time was the engine disconnected from the road wheels, giving sustained torque and smooth gear transition under full power.[5] Final drive to the axle was by spiral bevel gear as opposed to the more conventional worm assembly.

The Routemaster was developed from the outset to conform to long-standing LT flow production methods, in use at Chiswick and Aldenham Works and at local bus garages. Parts were standardised across the fleet as far as possible, and thus power, transmission, suspension, braking and ancillary units were interchangeable. As well as facilitating manufacture this expedited maintenance and enabled 'rapid disintegration'[6], a term coined by Durrant to refer to the fact that the body and mechanical units could be quickly separated for repair or overhaul.

The first Routemaster, a prototype designated RM1, was built at Chiswick Works in collaboration with Park Royal Vehicles Ltd. The mechanical units were built at Southall and supplied by the Associated Equipment Company (A.E.C.) Ltd. It was launched in a blaze of publicity and both the *Evening News* and the *Star* carried reports of its inaugural journey, a tour of the West End that took place on 31 January 1956. RM1 was subsequently put to work in passenger service with the object of highlighting any problems or defects before large-scale production got underway. In addition this represented an opportunity to gauge responses from the public. As such RM1 entered service on Wednesday 8 February 1956, operating on Route 2 (Golders Green–Crystal Palace) from Cricklewood Garage. It ran daily until the following autumn, when it returned to Chiswick Works to undergo further modifications. The timetables from this period still exist and are reproduced in this book, along with details from the Central Area Bus Map of 1956, which show starting and terminating points of the route.

Inside the bus, posters informed passengers that they were travelling on 'the forerunner of the future London bus', although one has to assume that most would have realised this, given the vehicle's novel appearance – and the fact that RM1's exterior advertising was replaced by signage proclaiming: 'THIS IS THE ROUTEMASTER, LONDON'S BUS OF THE FUTURE'. However, the poster also invited members of the public to write to London Transport's Public Relations Officer at 55 Broadway with comments relating to the Routemaster – which resulted in 61 letters being received in the period 8 February to 21 April 1956.

Given the almost universal acclaim the Routemaster subsequently attained in its long and distinguished service career, and the high esteem in which it is still held today, these early appraisals make for fascinating reading. The responses received may have dismayed Durrant, for although there were 75 appreciative comments there were also 76 criticisms. As becomes evident from a study of the table on pp.74-75, the criticisms focused on the inadequate ventilation provided by the windows and the admittedly erratic air flow/heating system, the poor resiliency of the seating, and the considerable noise generated by the engine transmission.

To London Transport's credit, they worked hard to address these and many other issues, and indeed a considerable number of modifications were made not only to RM1 but to three subsequent prototypes and to various production models. There were reliability problems and numerous faults to correct of varying degrees of seriousness, but in service the Routemaster would ultimately prove its worth – for London Transport, this was indeed the 'bus of the future'.

One of the main motivating factors for the creation of the Routemaster was the necessity to procure a replacement for London's ageing electrically powered trolleybus fleet. If the Routemaster represented the future, then the trolleybuses were firmly stuck in the past. First introduced in 1931, by the mid-1950s they were approaching the end of their service life and despite public affection for the 'trolleys', LT was keen to phase them out. Principally, the advantages of their replacement with diesel buses were that, as well as giving London a road public transport system running entirely on diesel, services would be given greater mobility in congested traffic; delays from power and other breakdowns would be minimised; and greater flexibility in routeing and integration of services could be offered.

It was calculated that this would lead to sizeable savings for London Transport, as is made clear in a document entitled 'The Use of Routemaster Buses', dated 21 June 1956. Herein it is noted that the projected cost of each individual Routemaster bus at this time actually exceeded that of its older, established cousin, the RT, but it is also pointed out that the Routemaster could carry 64 seated passengers, while the RT had seats for 56. Thus the cost per passenger actually worked out in favour of the Routemaster. The document also gives a fascinating assessment of the conditions pertaining to the operation of buses in London, thus providing the underlying rationale for the Routemaster design as well as outlining its key advantages over the operation of both trolleybuses and the RT type bus.

Production of the Routemaster vehicle was initially entrusted to A.E.C. Ltd., who manufactured the mechanical units, and Park Royal Vehicles Ltd., who manufactured the bus bodies. Both were part of the A.C.V. Group (Associated Commercial Vehicles Ltd.), from whom London Transport had agreed that at least 75 per cent of all new vehicles would be sourced. As such a batch of 850 buses were ordered, and by the end of 1959 they were rolling off the production line at a rate of around eight or nine per week.

An *A.E.C. Gazette* article from this period details their entry into service as part of Stage 4 of the trolleybus replacement programme, which commenced on 14 November 1959. They worked routes 5, 5A, 48 and 238 from the large former trolleybus depots at Poplar and West Ham, which had been converted for diesel bus operation. Routemasters also ran on route 23 (Barking–Marylebone), where services were increased in frequency, and on Sundays on an extended route 9.[7]

Early Routemaster production continued through 1960 and 1961, and the 1000th A.E.C. Routemaster was handed-over at a special ceremony held at Southall on 16 October 1961. This bus was assigned the registration number 100 BXL, a unique designation for a London Transport vehicle. It still survives in immaculate condition today.

Less than three weeks after 100 BXL was delivered, a new variant of the Routemaster went into service. This was the 30ft RML, an extended 72-seater version. The added capacity was achieved through the insertion of a 2ft 4in bay in the centre of the vehicle, and RMLs were thus conspicuous by the additional square windows that featured on both upper and lower decks. The integral construction of the Routemaster allowed for such alterations, and in total 524 of the longer wheelbase RML versions were built.

The Routemaster was further adapted in many other ways. This included, for example, the fitting of interior illuminated advertisements, as is recorded in a press release dated 29 November 1963. Advertising represented an additional and welcome source of revenue for London Transport. Adverts had long been familiar sights on the sides of London buses, first appearing in the days of horse-drawn omnibuses. In introducing external and internal illuminates posters Routemasters took this one stage further – although the spaces available for such advertising were still carefully prescribed.

The principal Routemaster vehicle types are described in a draft text written by Durrant himself. The standard RM and lengthened RML are covered in addition to the RMC and RCL 'coach' versions of the Routemaster, which were specially adapted to run the Green Line express services. Durrant also outlines the 30ft long forward-entrance Routemaster, designated RMF. The RMF did not ultimately see service with London Transport, but the 30ft prototype and an additional batch of sixty-five 27ft-long vehicles were purchased by British European Airways and used (with an additional luggage trailer) to ferry passengers to Heathrow and other airports. Gateshead bus company Northern General also took delivery of fifty 30ft RMF-type buses in May 1964.

'Routemaster Buses: Instructions for Drivers and Conductors' takes us full circle, back to those who knew this remarkable vehicle best: the drivers and conductors who worked the RM fleet on a daily basis. This instruction sheet dates from 1964 and is essentially a quick reference guide intended for LT employees newly assigned to the Routemaster. The text assumes a familiarity with the RT type, and it is logical to assume that it would therefore have been circulated widely among crews drawn from RT service. Undoubtedly the instructions would have been a useful item to have in the driver's cab or tucked away in the conductor's locker; a concise aide memoire for the series of procedures that were essential for elementary operation, whether starting the engine, leaving the vehicle or ventilating the interior saloons.

Neither are aspiring 'clippies' neglected with the inclusion of a user's guide to the Gibson bus ticket machine. This robust and versatile machine, introduced in October 1953, was the invention of George Gibson, a former superintendent of LT's ticket machine works at Effra Road, Brixton.[8] They proved their worth and became familiar sights on two-man operated buses for many years. The distinctive sound they made as the conductor issued his tickets remains, for many people, one of the most vivid memories of riding on a Routemaster.

Today the conductor has regrettably disappeared from London service, as two-man operation has been largely withdrawn, and the Routemaster serves London on a limited basis only. Specially preserved examples run on two designated 'heritage routes', serving on parts of routes number 9 (Kensington Olympia-Warwick Gardens—Trafalgar Square) and number 15 (Trafalgar Square–Tower Hill). It is still possible, therefore, to make a journey, albeit a short one, on board a red Routemaster bus in the capital.

The introduction of the much-heralded 'New Bus for London', however, will see the revival of the conductor and indeed the return of a bus that incorporates an open rear platform. The prototype vehicle is currently scheduled to enter service from 20 February 2012, and by May 2012 it is promised that eight will be in service, in time for the London 2012 Olympic Games. The 'New Bus for London' is the first bus designed specifically for London since the Routemaster, and is described as 'a contemporary take on the old Routemaster bus'[9]. Designed by Heatherwick Studio and built by Wrightbus, it features three doors and two staircases, and is powered by a hybrid diesel-electric drive system. When a conductor is on board passengers will be able to 'hop-on or off' via the open rear platform, for example in daytime service. When a conductor is not on board the platform can be closed off by a set of rear doors, which can be operated by the driver to facilitate one-man operation.

The 'New Bus for London' and its protracted development have been praised and castigated in equal measure. Ultimately how it performs in service should be the yardstick by which its success is measured. Yet even its development is irrefutable evidence, if any were needed, of the enduring appeal of the Routemaster. Moreover, it is testament to the attractive qualities and sound principles of the original design – a design that has rightly become a true icon of London.

Matthew Jones
London, January 2012

NOTES

1 National Register of Archives, Corporate Details, GB/NNAF/C96001
2 Fishman, Nina, *British Trade Unions and Industrial Politics*, Vol. I, pp.268-92 (Ashgate, 1999)
3 British Pathé, London, 08/08/1958, Canister 58/37, Film ID 1531.04, Tape PM1531
4 London Transport, Dept. of the Chief Mechanical Engineer (Road Services). Record of talk given to the Divisional and District Garage and Depot staff at Chiswick Works, 18 December 1957
5 London Transport Technical Information Sheet No. 10, November 1959
6 Record of talk (op. cit.)
7 Wagstaff, J. S. *The London Routemaster Bus*, Locomotion Papers No. 83 (Oakwood 1975), p.13
8 http://ronsroutemasters.webs.com/ticketmachines.htm (accessed 09/01/12)
9 'Designed For Londoners: Introducing London's latest landmark, the New Bus for London'. TfL information leaflet, 2011

LEARNING TO BE A BUS DRIVER

'The Bus Driver', J. Armstrong (1961)

If you live near a large bus garage you may sometimes have seen a drivers' training bus with ' L' plates at the front and rear and a group of men in rather new-looking uniforms inside. Some companies use a perfectly normal bus for this work, but others have fitted old buses with two sets of drivers' controls, one for the instructor and one for the learner. This arrangement is particularly suitable for teaching men who have not driven any kind of vehicle before.

Towards the end of their training course the learner-drivers always drive normal buses to help them to get used to the feeling of being alone at the front of the bus. Many bus drivers will tell you that their job is rather a lonely one.

We will join one of these travelling schools for drivers and find out some of the things the men are taught. On board the bus there are six learner-drivers and an experienced foreman-driver who is acting as their instructor. Four of the men have only just joined the bus company, and the other two are conductors who have applied to transfer to driving. All six men have their ordinary driving licences, and will shortly be taking the special driving test for the bus-drivers' licence. This is called the Public Service Vehicle Drivers' Licence; Public Service Vehicle is the rather long-winded official name for a bus or coach. A driver must have this licence in addition to his ordinary driving licence before he is allowed to take out a bus or coach on service. To show that he has passed the test and been given a licence, a bus driver has a red-bordered badge with a number on it that he must wear when on duty. You will usually see it on his coat lapel.

FORM P.S.V. 30/K

THE SOUTH-EASTERN TRAFFIC AREA,
SOUTHBRIDGE HOUSE,
SOUTHWARK BRIDGE ROAD,
LONDON, S.E.1.

LICENCE No. K 101401
BADGE No. KK 13204
DATE OF ISSUE 7/9/59

LICENCE TO DRIVE A PUBLIC SERVICE VEHICLE.

ROAD TRAFFIC ACTS, 1930 to 1956.

THIS LICENCE is issued by the TRAFFIC COMMISSIONERS for the SOUTH-EASTERN TRAFFIC AREA and authorises—

HANTS

*Strike out the words which follow if not appropriate.

to drive a public service vehicle* of the type or types shown in the schedule below.

SCHEDULE.

Type or types of public service vehicles which the licensee is licensed to drive.

ALL TYPES

This licence shall have effect as from 28/8/59
and shall continue in force for three years from that date.

Fee 3/-

Signature of licensee (see Note 1)
(In ink.)

NOTES.

(1) The licensee must sign this licence in ink in the space provided above immediately on receiving it; but must not write anything else on it.

(2) The licensee must notify the Commissioners of any change of address within 7 days of such change.

(3) This licence does not absolve the licensee from the obligation to obtain a licence to drive under Part I of the Act of 1930. The latter licence has a stiff cover in which this licence when folded into six can conveniently be kept.

(4) If this licence covers all types of single deck public service vehicles, the holder may drive heavy goods vehicles without a special licence for that purpose under Section 31 of the Road Traffic Act, 1934.

(5) Any inquiries regarding this licence should be addressed to the Commissioners at the address given at the top.

A Public Service Vehicle Driver's licence. The words 'all types' show that the holder may drive any kind of bus or coach, single-decker or double-decker

Before our six learners start off on-their final training run, the foreman-driver reminds them of some of the things that will be watched with particular care when they take their test. The hand-signals that they make must be given clearly with the whole hand and forearm, not just

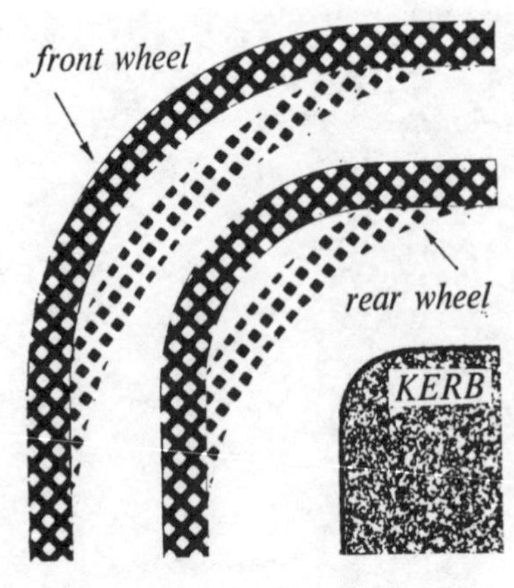

How the wheels of a bus 'cut corners'

with the tips of their fingers. They must also remember the length and width of the bus, and avoid cutting their corners and letting the back wheels mount the pavement.

As each learner-driver has his turn at the wheel, the foreman-driver watches him and afterwards comments on the way he handled the bus. He makes each man practice such things as drawing up at a bus stop with the platform just level with the post, reversing the bus round a sharp corner into a narrow side road, and keeping to various speeds without constantly glancing at the speedometer. He also makes them take the bus along a tree-lined street to remind them that a double-decker must not be driven too close to the roadside. The camber of the road can cause the top deck to lean far enough towards the pavement to receive damage from other overhead obstructions, and the driver must keep a look-out for tall lamp-posts set close to the kerb.

When they arrive back at the garage, the foreman-driver tells his class that they are ready to take the official driving test, and he gives them a final piece of advice. 'When you are driving a bus,' he says, 'never forget for a moment that there may be sixty or more passengers behind you. It is your job to give them a safe and comfortable journey, so never take risks, and always drive as smoothly as if your own family were on the bus.'

In addition to the driving test for the Public Service Vehicle Licence, there is a strict medical examination by a doctor. No one can get a bus driver's licence unless he has eyesight, hearing, and health and strength that are up to the right standard. Good eyesight is necessary because drivers are always having to judge distances in which to stop or overtake, and they also have to drive at night and keep going in foggy weather. Colour blindness is sometimes discovered during the medical examination and the man concerned may not be passed fit for bus driving. Coloured lights of various kinds form many of the signals and warnings on our roads, and a driver must be able to recognise them instantly if he is to drive with safety.

Bus driving needs a man of good general health and reasonable strength. The steering and other controls of a heavy vehicle need much greater effort than those of a private car and, as the foreman-driver reminded his class, a bus driver is responsible for the safety of a large number of people, and that can be tiring as well.

The effect of road camber: if the bus were driven too close to the kerb, the roof would hit the lamp-post

The driving test for the Public Service Vehicle Licence is set by an official from the Ministry of Transport. He is called a Vehicle Examiner, and we shall see later on that he does in fact examine vehicles as well as supervise driving tests. The route he has chosen for the test includes examples of all the difficulties that are normally found by drivers on a bus route. There is a section uphill and another downhill, both as steep as he can find in the neighbourhood. There are also some narrow roads, sharp corners, road junctions with halt signs, busy streets with zebra crossings, and so on.

If you were one of the learner-drivers taking the test you would meet the Examiner at the depot and a normal double-deck bus (with the screens showing private) would be provided for you. Before the test began the Examiner would tell you the route he had chosen, and then he and the foreman-driver would climb aboard. The foreman-driver is coming along just in case anything goes badly wrong and someone is needed to drive the bus back to the garage.

Feeling a little nervous, you would probably find yourself driving very slowly at first, but after one or two smooth gear-changes you would gain confidence. All the time you would remember the Examiner sitting in the bus watching you and making notes. Are you making your hand signals properly? Have you remembered to glance in your rear-view mirrors occasionally to see if any vehicles are behind you and wanting to overtake? As you approach the steep downhill section of the route the Examiner will expect you to change to third gear. That helps to take the strain off the brakes, because the bus cannot go as fast in third gear as it can in top. When you have to stop at traffic lights you must wait for the green light before you start again, remembering that the amber light is only the signal to get ready.

Those are some of the points that the Examiner will watch, and his main concern will be whether you are driving the bus safely.

The Highway Code contains the principles you must follow for safety on the road, and if the Examiner finds you do not obey them he will not pass you fit for bus driving. Nor will he pass you if you give him a jerky and uncomfortable ride or make the bus sway by going too fast round corners.

One important part of the test takes place on the uphill section. About half-way up the Examiner rings the bell for you to stop the bus, and comes round to the cab to tell you to start away again up the hill, being very careful not to let the bus roll back. Some Examiners are said to put an empty matchbox behind one wheel of the bus for this part of the test. If the bus rolls back even an inch it will squash the matchbox, and the driver will find he has failed the test! There is quite a knack in releasing the hand-brake and the clutch pedal together so that the bus moves smoothly forward up the hill. If the bus was allowed to roll back it would alarm the passengers and a serious accident could be caused should a car be waiting close behind it.

A little farther on the Examiner stops the bus again and asks you to reverse it into a side turning. To do this successfully with a long vehicle is more difficult than you might imagine. It is important to finish up with the bus neatly beside the kerb, and not too far from it.

Finally the Examiner will ask you questions on the Highway Code. The first one might be about traffic lights; see if you can answer it correctly. 'When only the amber light is shining what will be the next colour to light up?' Next a question about overtaking: 'Normally you may only overtake to the right of the vehicle in front, but what are the exceptions to this rule?' Then you might be asked to describe the road signs that indicate a hospital and a level crossing, or to explain the difference between the halt and slow signs where there is a major road ahead. Finally, there is a question about turning right. 'If you are about to make a right turn into another road and there is a line of traffic approaching, so that you have to halt while it passes, where exactly would you stop and wait?' The correct answer is that you should stop just to the left of the centre of the road, so that cars behind you can pass safely on your left and are not held up.

If you ride a bicycle you should know the answer to these questions without having to look them up; the Highway Code is just as important to a cyclist as to a bus driver.

When the test is over the Examiner tells the foreman-driver the names of the men who have passed, and next day they report for duty at the bus garage.

Before he can start driving on service, the newly-licensed man must get to know the routes, the positions of the stops, and the speeds necessary for good time-keeping over the different sections, and to do this he takes one or two journeys as a passenger on service buses driven by experienced men.

As well as learning the routes, the new drivers are given a number of rules to read and learn. One of these is that the first driver of the day on each bus must test the brakes before starting on service. Another rule is that the driver is always responsible for seeing that the radiator of his bus is filled with water. There is also a set of instructions on what a driver must do if he is involved in an accident, and another important rule refers to the ' Drivers' Report Book', which is kept on a desk outside the foreman's office. As each bus is brought into the garage at the end of its day's work, the driver must enter in the Report Book any fault he has noticed about the vehicle, so that the garage staff can tell which buses need urgent attention before they go out on the road again.

When the newly-licensed drivers are ready to take buses out on service, the foreman-driver adds their names to the duty fist that is posted up in the garage. He reminds them that it is part of their job to be punctual and to be certain of the details of their day's work. These details are sometimes quite complicated, and may include instructions

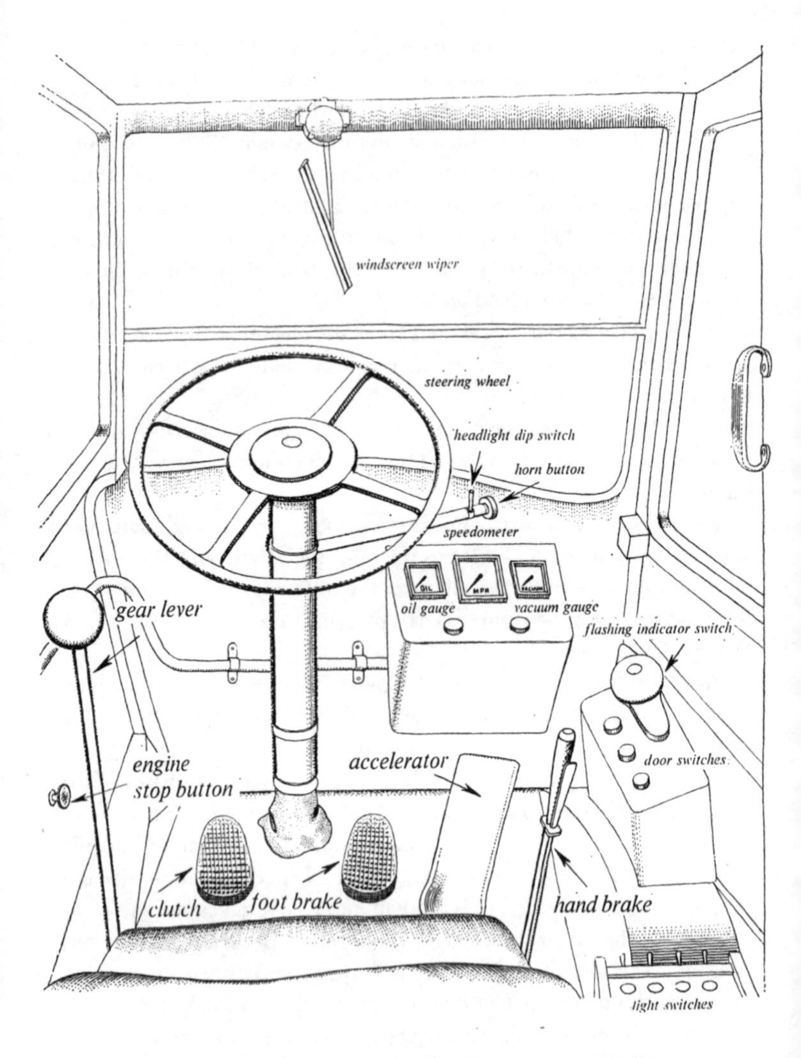

The bus driver's cab and controls. Note that the Routemaster's cab differed in several significant ways from the generic type shown here. For example, the clutch was eliminated, the handbrake was moved to the driver's left-hand side and the gear lever was mounted on the steering column

about connections with other services, or special destination screens, which would cause serious inconvenience if they were forgotten.

A typical day's work for a bus driver would appear on the notice-board. Bus crews call their day's work their 'duty', and in a big bus garage there would be over a hundred duties, to be carried out every weekday, and more than half of them on Sundays as well. A staff of schedules clerks works them out, taking great care that there is a crew allotted to every journey in the time-table, and also that the drivers never work longer than the maximum hours allowed by law. For example, bus drivers may not work for more than five and a half hours without a break of at least half an hour, and they must normally have at least ten hours off duty between the end of one day's work and the start of the next. The schedules clerks have to take these restrictions and usually other special instructions into account in carrying out their highly skilled work.

In some garages the crews like to have as much variety as possible in each duty, so the schedules do not require them to work on one service all the time. In other cases, particularly where all the services are very much the same, the crews actually prefer to remain on one route. In some fleets each crew works the same duty for a week and in others they change duties every day. Similarly, it is not everywhere that drivers always work with the same conductor, though it has many advantages if they do. Driver and conductor have to work as a team, and the most successful teams are often those who understand each other best from long experience of working together.

BEHIND THE SCENES

'The Bus Driver', J. Armstrong (1961)

Some bus garages are so small that they only hold a single bus, but others can accommodate over a hundred. The small garages are usually to be found in villages at the end of country bus routes. They are used simply to keep a bus under cover at night and are known as dormy (from 'dormitory') sheds. The larger garages are usually in big towns, and those holding thirty or more vehicles will have an engineering staff to attend to maintenance and repairs. Work on the buses goes on day and night in some garages, though this does not mean that buses are always having breakdowns. Many of us think of mechanics as people to be called in when something goes wrong, but in a bus fleet the mechanics, or fitters as they are called, spend most of their time on work which is carefully planned to prevent breakdowns happening at all. This is known as maintenance: they are maintaining the buses in good order. The engineers in charge of the fleet know from experience that when a bus has covered a certain mileage the chance of a breakdown or of faulty operation becomes much greater, so they work out a detailed programme for the inspection and regular replacement of nearly every mechanical part. The programme varies according to the type of bus, but in a typical fleet maintenance is based on each vehicle having a thorough inspection about every eight thousand miles. These inspections, which are known as docks, take about a day to carry out, or longer if repairs are found to be necessary.

Looking into a typical large bus garage during the middle of the day, you might be surprised at the lack of noise and the small number of men to be seen at work, although there will probably be twenty or thirty buses standing in the garage. Only four or five of these are undergoing repairs and maintenance. The rest are rush-hour reliefs which have to be kept to cater for the crowds of people who travel to work between eight and nine o'clock in the morning and go home again between five and six o'clock in the evening. For the rest of the day there is no work for these extra buses, so they have to stand idle in the garage.

Beside the entrance doors stands a pair of fuelling standards, rather like the petrol pumps in a filling station. They are placed conveniently to refill the buses as they return to the garage after their day's work. The fuel is kept in great underground tanks, and the fuelling standards contain powerful pumps which can draw up the thirty gallons needed to refill a bus in a very short time. To prevent waste the filling-nozzle is fitted with a device that automatically shuts off the flow of fuel as soon as the tank is full.

A few yards farther inside the garage there is a rectangle marked out in white paint on the floor, and hanging from the roof above it is the bus-washing machine. This consists of an aluminium frame carrying revolving brushes that exactly fit round the outside of a bus. The brushes are driven by an electric motor, and the frame is also fitted with a water-pipe with holes drilled in it at intervals.

In the evening after each returning bus has been refuelled it is driven forward and carefully parked inside the white rectangle. Then the washing machine is switched on and lowered round the bus. As it descends it sprays water all over the roof and sides, and the spinning brushes quickly remove the dust and dirt picked up during the day's run. When the washing machine has been lowered almost to ground level the controls are reversed and it is hoisted up again ready for the next bus. It takes less than two minutes to wash each bus in this way, a great saving in time, although the cleaners still have to finish off various parts of the bus by hand, and sweep out the inside. They work throughout the night, moving steadily along the rows of parked buses and wearing special face-masks to avoid inhaling the clouds of dust stirred up by their brooms.

From time to time powerful vacuum cleaners are used to give the upholstery of the seats a spring clean.

The underneath of the buses is also cleaned occasionally, but this is such a dirty job that it is not done inside the garage. The bus is raised up to a height of about five feet by a hydraulic lift and the underside is hosed with a powerful jet of steam that soon loosens and removes the caked and oily mud that gathers there.

At the far end of the garage are the inspection pits where most of the maintenance work is carried out. These pits are made deep enough to allow a man to stand upright when attending to a job underneath a bus, and they are fitted with lights that shine upwards to illuminate the work. At one end the pits open out into a workshop where the fitters keep their tools and equipment. Much of the fitters' work is concerned with the inspection and replacement of parts which have completed a certain mileage in service. For example, the fuel pumps on a certain type of diesel engine are changed after fifty thousand miles, and this is done whether there appears to be anything wrong with the pumps or not. When a pump has been removed after remaining in service for this mileage (which represents over a year's work) it is returned to the Company's central workshops. There it is dismantled and inspected. Worn parts are replaced and the pump is then put together again, carefully tested, and fitted to another engine. The same principle is followed with most of the other mechanical parts of the bus. The central workshops are equipped with all kinds of machinery and can undertake very big jobs such as rebuilding bus bodies and reconditioning engines. Each bus would be sent there for a complete overhaul about every three years.

Perhaps the largest repair job to be carried out in an ordinary bus garage would be to change a complete engine weighing about one and a half tons, and at the other extreme are the small but still important routine jobs of oiling and greasing.

In addition to the fitters who work on the engines and chassis there are electricians to look after the many items of electrical equipment such as batteries, lights, heaters, and bells that are fitted in buses. There is also a staff of specially trained men whose job it is to see that the tyres are kept in good condition and pumped up to the correct pressures. In a one-hundred-bus garage they would have six hundred tyres to look after, and extra ones in the case of coaches, for which spare tyres are a legal requirement.

Regular attention is the theme of all the important work done by the engineering staff. They often have to carry out their work knowing that the bus will soon be badly needed for service, but however urgent the work they can never forget that a mistake on their part could result in a serious accident. If it were not for their skill and care the drivers would be unable to keep up the remarkable record of safety for which they are well known.

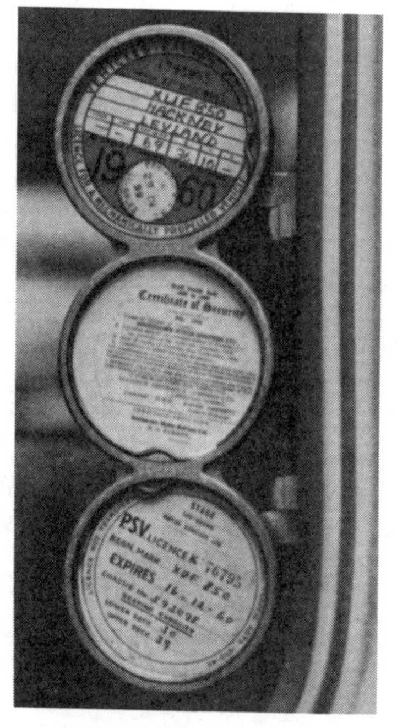

Displayed in the cab window are the 'Road Fund' licence (at the top), the Certificate of Insurance and the Public Service Vehicle licence which every British bus and coach must carry when in service

At least once a year each bus is given an official Ministry of Transport inspection. This is carried out by the Vehicle Examiner, whom we last met testing new bus drivers. He pays particular attention to the steering mechanism and the brakes, which are so important from the point of view of safety, but if he were to find anything wrong with any part of the bus he could order it to be kept off the road until it had been repaired to his satisfaction. But the routine attention that the buses receive is so thorough that this seldom happens.

The man in charge of the maintenance staff in the garage is the Depot Engineer. From his office overlooking the inspection pits he plans and controls the work that is done on the buses. His clerks keep records that give him a kind of mechanical history of each bus, showing the mileage it has covered and when it was last docked. Most buses in timetabled service run over a thousand miles in a week, and the records are very necessary to enable the next maintenance job for each bus to be planned in advance and to ensure that none of the details is overlooked. Another set of records is necessary for the various licences and certificates, of which you can see three displayed in the cab window of every bus. They are the Public Service Vehicle Licence, the Certificate of Insurance, and the Motor Taxation Licence. In addition to these records, others are kept so that each driver can be told when it is time to renew either of his own two licences.

Built on to the front of the garage and facing the street you will often find a booking-office, and at the larger garages there is also likely to be an office for the Depot Manager and his staff.

The clerks in the booking-office must be experts on the company's time-tables so that they can quickly answer questions from people who want to know the time of the next bus, or the last bus, or the first bus on Sundays, on their particular route.

There will also be passengers coming in to the office to book tickets for express coach services and excursions. One reason why many people like to travel by coach rather than by train is that they know their ticket guarantees them a seat and they will not have to stand. A careful record has to be kept of all the coach tickets sold. When the booking-clerk makes out a ticket for a coach passenger he fills in the date, the time of the journey, and the name of the stop where the passenger wants to board the coach. He copies these details on to a seating plan of the coach called a 'chart'. There is a separate chart kept in the booking-office for every coach journey for months ahead, and by looking at the entries on the right one a booking-clerk can always tell whether there are seats available. When the coach is due to leave the details on the chart are given to the driver to show him how many passengers he should have and where they will join the coach. Very occasionally, even in the best-run booking-offices, extra passengers are booked by mistake although the chart shows the coach is already full. When this happens the bookings are said to have 'gone over the top', and it is one of the worst mistakes a booking-clerk can make. It means that an extra coach and driver must be found—usually at the last moment—to deal with the over-load. But this will be done rather than leave anyone behind.

Among the people who call are passengers who have left things on the buses, and next door to the booking-office is the lost-property store. Here are rows of wooden shelves all round the walls, crowded with gloves, shoes, school-caps, umbrellas, attache cases, and all kinds of other things. They are all carefully labelled with the date and the route on which they were found, and the name of the conductor who handed them in. Before a passenger can reclaim his lost property he has to pay a small fee, of which part is given to the conductor, by law, as a reward for finding the article and handing it in.

The oddest things are sometimes left on buses. You would not think that on a short bus journey anyone could forget a pair of leg-irons, or a set of false teeth, or a bag containing over £100 worth of jewellery, yet these are some of the things that have been found on buses, and even the most valuable articles are not always claimed. Unclaimed lost property is kept in store for at least three months and is then offered to the conductor who handed it in, before being put up for sale.

In one of the larger offices behind the booking-hall clerks are busy counting and recording the fare-money paid in by the conductors as they go off duty. The total of each conductor's cash has to agree with the total value of the tickets he has sold to his passengers. Modern types of conductors' ticket machines automatically add up the fares as the tickets are issued. There is a picture of one of these machines and the kind of ticket it issues overleaf. At the beginning of the conductor's period of duty the ticket machine is loaded with a narrow roll of plain paper sufficient for about seven hundred tickets. Every time the conductor takes a fare he sets the amount and other information on the controls of the machine. Then he turns the handle and the machine stamps the required details on the end of the ticket roll and feeds it out of a slot to be torn off and handed to the passenger. Each time the conductor turns the handle the machine automatically adds the amount of the fare to the totals shown on the counters. For example, a 1s. 3d. ticket issued from the machine would cause the 1s. counter to move on by one, and the 1d. counter to move on by three. A 2½d. ticket causes the 1d. counter to move on by two and a half, and so on. The machine also prints a serial number on each ticket that is issued, and automatically adds one to the number ready for the next ticket. Some of these ingenious machines even take copies of every ticket issued, and others have a spare counter which can be set to record the number of tickets issued at any particular fare.

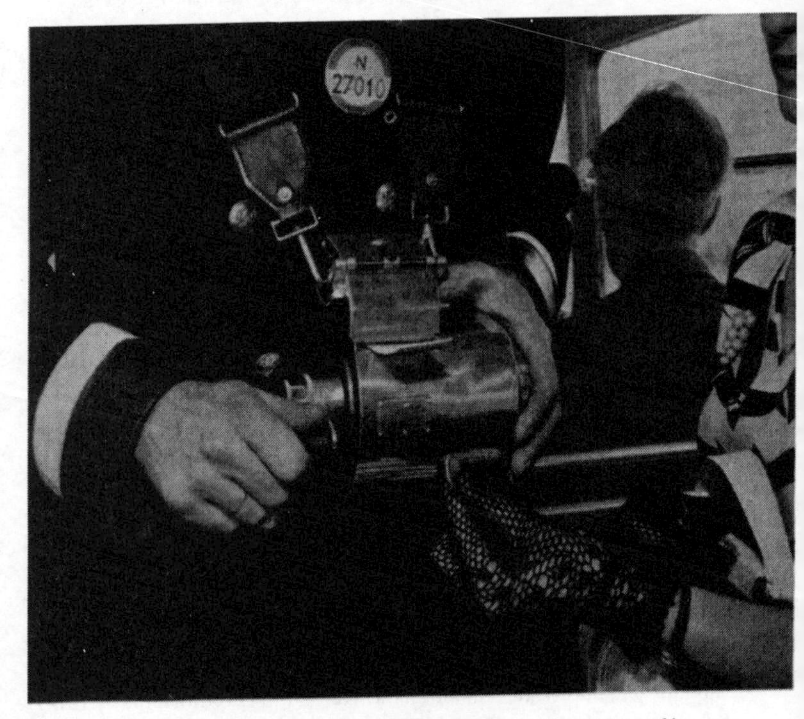

A London Transport bus conductor issuing a ticket from a Gibson ticket machine

TIMETABLES AND DUTY SCHEDULES

'Timetable and Duty Schedule Compilation' [Road Passenger Transport], J. F. Turner (1946)

INTRODUCTION – GENERAL SURVEY OF WORK INVOLVED IN THE PREPARATION OF TIME AND DUTY SCHEDULES – DEFINITION OF TERMS

The Timetable and its related Duty Schedule is the basis of every passenger Service and may be considered the 'theory' of actual operation. The value of any theory can best be gauged by applying a practical test, and there is no doubt that any imperfection of Timetable or of Duty Schedule will become very evident as soon as the service is put into operation. If adverse criticism is to be avoided, there is, therefore, every need for the utmost care in the preparation of the Timetable and Duty Schedule of each Service and this will demand not only accuracy as regards the mass of figures involved, but also the adoption of sound principles of construction.

The revenue-earning capacity of a Service to a large extent is dependent upon a well-planned Timetable adequately serving the passengers' requirements at the time they exist and avoiding the operation of any unnecessary journeys when such facilities are not in strong demand. It is worth while to observe, however, that whilst such a Timetable is an important factor in the acquisition of revenue, the Duty Schedule, which provides the hours of duty performed by the Platform Staff, will function in an opposite direction, in that it will control the expenditure of a large proportion of such income.

The true value of a Service of high earning-capacity, therefore, would be perceptibly diminished if the associated Duty Schedule should prove wasteful and hence there exists a very close and important relationship between these two functions.

It may be well at this stage to indicate in sequence the main functions performed in the Schedules Office of a large Passenger Transport Undertaking, and these may conveniently be summarized as follows: —

(1) The preparation of the Timetable (or Time Schedule).
(2) The abstraction therefrom of the times of the journeys performed by each vehicle in service and the entry of such journeys upon Time Cards for use upon each respective vehicle.
(3) The further abstraction of the times of all journeys for all Routes serving selected Traffic points for use of the Regulating Officials and Road Control Staff.
(4) The preparation of the Daily Duty Schedule.
(5) The preparation of the Weekly Rota of Duties.
(6) The Compilation of Schedule Analyses and Statistics.

One result of the lack of standardization of method and practice in the industry is the many operational terms now in use, the meanings of some of which are synonymous, whilst the interpretation of others will vary in accord with local usage. Hence it is essential, if misunderstanding is to be avoided, clearly to define the meaning of the terms used within these pages. A list of such definitions appears hereunder: —

Duty. The work scheduled daily for the performance of each individual crew, which, in addition to the amount of "duty" performed upon the vehicle, will include all "duty" incidental thereto such as signing on and off duty, travelling between the garage and relief-point. "Duties" may, or may not be provided with an unpaid period of "Relief" and according to whether or not such a break of "duty" occurs they will be described as "Split" or "Straight-through" duties respectively.

Duty Spell. One of the two portions or "Spells" of work comprising a Split Duty—separated from the other "Spell" by the period of "relief."

Duty Schedule. A Schedule showing the details of work performed daily upon indicated buses by each crew—together, with other incidental "duty"—and providing in entirety for the operation of the service scheduled on the related Timetable.

Duty Rota (or *Roster*). A Schedule of the daily "Duties" performed throughout each week by each crew, arranged to provide work for 6 days and a weekly rotation of the "Rest-days."

Duty Hours. The total amount of Duty-time scheduled for daily or weekly performance by individual crews inclusive of all "Time Allowances" for such purposes as "Signing on and off duty", "Travel-time" between garage and relief-point (if any) but excluding the unpaid period of "Relief."

Duty Classification. The classification of Duties as "Early," "Middle" or "Late" turns, in accordance with the time of the commencement and/or conclusion of the Duty, each "class" being subject to local definition.

Frequency of Service. The Interval of Service (or Headway) provided on the Timetable may be expressed in minutes (i.e. Frequency of 6 minutes) or by "Buses per hour" (i.e. 10 buses per hour)—the former tending to indicate a stricter regularity of service than is implied by the latter.

Garage Runs. Journeys operated between the garage and the point of contact with the line of route (in some instances not providing for the carriage of passengers).

Mileage.

Scheduled Service Mileage. The recorded amount of revenue-earning "Service" mileage scheduled for operation upon the Timetable.

Lost Mileage.The amount of Scheduled Service Mileage not operated by reason of operational default.

Excess Mileage. The amount of mileage, in excess of that scheduled upon the Timetable, operated in emergency.

Actual Service Mileage. The recorded figure of Scheduled Service Mileage duly adjusted as to any lost or excess mileage incurred.

Dead Mileage. Mileage scheduled for operation upon the Timetable but not providing for the carriage of passengers.

Normal Hours or Slack Hours. The periods of the Traffic-day other than "peak" (or rush) hours when the traffic conditions are "normal" or unintensified.

Peak Hours or Rush Hours. The periods of the Traffic-day when the Service is augmented to cater for increased passenger loads.

Relief-period. The unpaid period of a "Split" Duty scheduled between the two "Spells" of duty and provided as a "break" in which to obtain refreshment.

Relief-point (or *Change-over-point*). The point upon the line of Route where an exchange of crews is effected.

Rest-day. The day of the week upon which each man in turn is not required to perform a daily Duty, often arranged to "rotate" in a period of successive weeks.

Running-time, or journey-time. The amount of time provided on the Timetable for the operation of single or return journeys between the Terminals and between intermediate timing-points which, for the present purpose, is inclusive of the time allowed for "Terminal working" but exclusive, of "Stand-time."

Running Number. The number assigned to each vehicle required to operate the service for identification purposes.

Roster— see "Duty Rota."

Stand-time or Layover Time. Time scheduled at the Terminal—mainly to ensure regularity of service.

Spreadover of Duty. The length of time—inclusive of the period of Relief and all Time Allowances—calculated from the time of commencement to the time of conclusion of Duty.

Terminal Working. A short circuitous route followed by the vehicle at the conclusion of a journey to effect the necessary turnabout and usually essential at congested Traffic points. The limits of the "Terminal working" may be defined by the points selected for the "setting-down" and "picking-up" of passengers, between which it is usual for no passengers to be carried. Located between these points is the "Stand," providing accommodation for the vehicles whilst awaiting the scheduled time of departure upon their next journey. For the present purposes the time involved in operating the "Terminal working" is included in "Running time."

Time Allowances. Allowances of time included in the Duty-hours of every Duty for the performance of duties incidental to the work performed upon the vehicle (i.e. Signing on and off duty, Travel-time, etc.).

THE TIMETABLE (I)—ITS FORM AND THE BASIC FACTORS OF CONSTRUCTION

There are numerous forms of Timetables in use, ranging between the simple and the complex, and of varying degrees of intricacy and of clarity. In large measure the form is dependent upon the characteristics of the route operated and the type of service provided—for if the operation is complex it is more difficult, but not impossible, to achieve clarity in the construction of the Timetable. The main requirement of every Timetable is an indication in as clear and concise form as possible of all the essential details of the operation so that the times of all the journeys; the frequency of service provided between all points; the times at which changes of frequency and of running-time are effected, and the identification of the vehicle performing each journey, readily is ascertainable.

A simple Service operating at a constant frequency throughout the Traffic-day between two Terminals will present no difficulty, but when an augmented service is provided at certain periods over only part, or over more than one part of the whole Route, or should deviations from the normal Route occur, then the avoidance of complication is less easy of attainment. For general use, the Timetable should show all journey-times at all points of the Route in a strictly chronological order but whether the times are arranged perpendicularly (as is the practice adopted in the published Railway Timetables) or in horizontal alignment (perhaps the better for our present purpose) is not so important a requirement as the need to enter every journey-time in order of time.

For certain official, purposes, however, it may prove advantageous to be able to see at a glance details of the operations performed by each individual vehicle. The computation of the mileage scheduled for Operation by each individual vehicle and the abstraction of certain other information required by the Engineering Staff and Traffic Officials are but some of the purposes served by the Timetable, and it would facilitate the use of the Timetable for such incidental purposes if the operation of each vehicle could be shown in horizontal alignment. Even from certain aspects of Duty Schedule compilation the factors required to be considered are more apparent if this method is adopted, but whilst all these requirements are adequately met without difficulty in the case of simple, straightforward operation, in dealing with a service of a more complex character it may involve sacrificing the strict chronological entry of every journey-time. Within certain limits, however, it is possible to devise means of preserving the chronological order of times and at the same time of providing a not too involved method of tracing the individual operations performed by each vehicle in service.

In order to discriminate between these two possible forms of Timetable—serving two distinct purposes—it is suggested the term "Timetable" should be applied only to that form upon which is shown, the journey-time in a strict order of time, whilst that form which is required for the more "official" uses, and is unsuitable for publication without adjustment, might be described as a "Time Schedule."

It is, however, the former of these forms (the Timetable) with which we at present are concerned, and all examples which appear in the following pages will conform to that form. Although these examples, for reasons of economy of space, may not show times at intermediate Traffic-points, other than those at which a short operation terminates, it should be mentioned that in practice it should prove an aid to the maintenance of correct time-keeping if provision is made on the Timetables for the times of journeys to be entered at certain selected intermediate points even though no vehicles are scheduled to turn short at such points.

There are four important basic factors which require special attention in considering the construction of all Timetables. These are:—

(1) The frequency of service to be provided throughout the Traffic-day.
(2) The times of operation of the first and last journeys and the time at which any change of frequency of service is to be effected.
(3) The running-time to be provided between the terminals and between the intermediate Traffic-points.
(4) The amount of Stand-time to be allocated to each Terminal or Turning-point.

The importance attached to these factors will become more apparent as progress is made in our studies, but the following notes will assist the Student at this stage to appreciate their significance:—

(1) The Frequency of Service

Whilst the determination of the frequency of service to be provided is not usually a responsibility of the Schedules Office, it may be stated that this factor is decided after full consideration of the Public requirements either expressed on their behalf through the usual channels, or gauged from a study of the earning-capacity of the Route, an examination of the passenger loading checks and a knowledge of the passenger-traffic conditions as reported by Traffic Observers or Operating Officials. The construction of every Timetable is based upon a regularity of service interval, although to meet an acute congestion of traffic occurring at short specified periods and in order to maintain special journeys timed to connect with trains or to provide for the interchange of passengers with other Routes, such regularity may temporarily be disturbed. The point is, however, that the basis of all construction is regularity of service.

When dealing with a "complex" Timetable providing for a service of varying intensity over different sections of the whole Route it is necessary to decide over which section the irregular service—resulting from vehicles turning short at an intermediate point—shall be scheduled. This decision will be influenced by the relative length of the respective sections of Route and the prevailing passenger-traffic conditions experienced thereon.

This point may best be explained, by an example :—

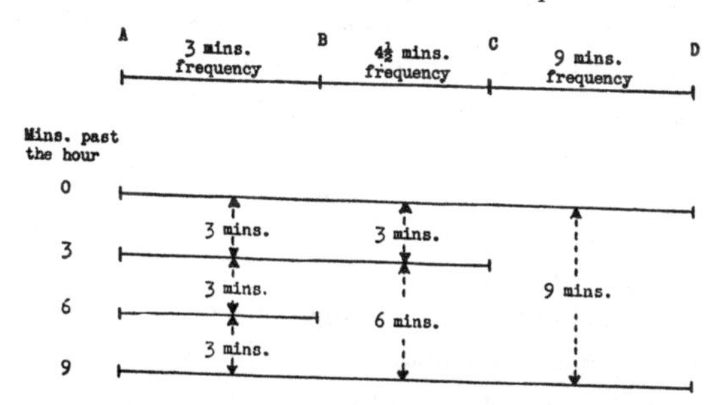

Let the line A–D represent the full extent of a Route and the points. B and C shown thereon indicate intermediate turning-points to which operate services additional to that provided on the through-route between A and D. If the service provided from A to B, to C and to D are each of 9 mins. frequency and are timed to depart from A at regular intervals of 3 mins. then it is clear that, by virtue of the absence between B and D of the vehicles which terminate at B, the resultant frequency between B and C is irregular—consisting of intervals alternatively of 3 mins. and 6 mins. Should the condition between these points (B and C) be such as to demand a more even interval of service, then this may be achieved only by distorting the existing regularity of interval (3 mins.) provided between A and B as under :—

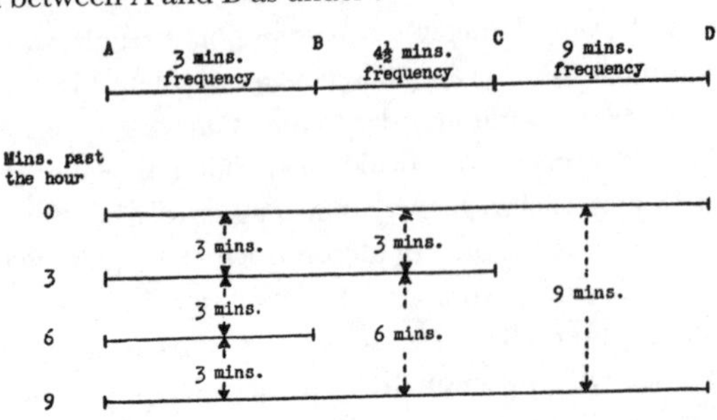

In the drafting of a Timetable for such a service as the above, it is necessary to consider the effect upon operational conditions created by an uneven frequency of service—for the vehicle which forms the wider interval of service will, of course, tend to carry the heavier load. Hence, endeavour should be made to ensure that the shorter interval occurs between the vehicle operating the short journey (to B) and the vehicle proceeding to the further Terminal (D) as shown above, rather than the reverse, for by so doing a smaller number of short-distance passengers will be present at A to board the through-vehicle upon its departure to D and hence the accommodation available thereon for the long-distance passengers will be greater.

Attention also must be given to the subject of the interworking of services over common sections of route, for it is obviously desirable that when an important section of route of one Service also is covered by the operation of another Service, attempt should be made to achieve a combined frequency as evenly spaced as possible in both directions of travel. The possibility of achieving this aim is dependent upon the respective frequency of service provided upon each route, for unless they are the same, perfect interworking is not possible, although in certain circumstances the avoidance of clashing of times will be possible. It should be added that even when there exists a common frequency upon each Service the even spacing of the journey-times in both directions cannot always be assured.

(2) First and last journey-times and times of Changes in Frequency

It is always of advantage (particularly from a Publicity point of view) to maintain existing times of the early and late operations upon successive Timetables except when evidence justifies an alteration. Such evidence will, of course, be forthcoming from the same sources which influenced the decision reached as to the frequency of service to be provided, and the same may be said as regards the time at which a change of frequency of service is required.

(3) Running-time

There can be no doubt that adequacy of Running-time is essential from all aspects of operation—but it also is necessary to realize that an excess of Running-time is as detrimental to good operation as an insufficiency thereof. It must be conceded that those responsible for the operation of the services should be permitted to decide the amount of running-time necessary to maintain the services they control, for with their wide and intimate knowledge of the local conditions they should be in a position to determine with some degree of accuracy where a variation of speed is required to meet any existing congestion upon the route and to ensure satisfactory time-keeping, but should doubt exist, it always will be possible to arrange for a test to be taken. Whatever amount of Running-time between defined points is decided upon this will be but an average figure considered sufficient to meet any variation of running consequent upon periodical road congestion or caused by an uneven distribution or irregular flow of passenger-traffic. In the construction of the Timetable, it is important to realise that in all circumstances the agreed amount must consistently be applied and no variation therefrom can be permitted except when a definite change has been authorised.

(4) Stand-time

The main purpose for which Stand-time is provided—at least in theory—is for the correction of any irregularity of service or departure from "Scheduled" times which may occur, but in practice other reasons may be prescribed. The length of the route, or to be more correct, the amount of Running-time necessary to operate the respective journeys, is perhaps the dominating factor concerned in deciding the amount and the allocation of Stand-time, for it may be accepted that the longer the route the greater will be the possibility and the extent of erratic running and hence the greater will be the need for an adequate amount of Stand-time for the correction of any such irregularity as may occur and for the provision of a "break" in which the crews may have an opportunity to "stretch their legs".

For the purpose of the demonstrations in the construction of Timetables to be undertaken at a later stage [not included here], it is highly desirable to fix a standard and to ensure a reasonable amount of Stand-time and in the examples subsequently to be given it is therefore proposed to adopt, as the minimum amount to be allocated between the two Terminals, a standard of 5% of the Running-time scheduled for each return journey.

In actual practice the accommodation available for the standing of vehicles at the Terminals or Turning-points may be subject to rigid restriction and hence there can be no guarantee that the amount of Stand-time it is desired to allow always can be scheduled upon every occasion; but in many instances it will prove possible to compensate for any deficiency of Stand-time at one Terminal by a corresponding increase at the other Terminal.

In providing for the satisfactory interworking of services operating over common sections of route, it also may be necessary to adjust the amount of Stand-time between the Terminals and even, upon occasion, to provide an amount of Stand-time, at one or both of the Terminals, in excess of that recognized as adequate, in order to achieve this object, but it ever is necessary to consider the extent of the accommodation available at each Terminal. In considering the possibility of a variation of total Stand-time, however, it is necessary to emphasize that any contemplated increase (or for that matter any decrease) of total Stand-time varying the standard accepted as necessary for operation of the Service, must consist of a multiple of the frequency of the service operated.

Daily Duty Schedules

MONDAY TO FRIDAY				
Duty No.	Report Time	Finishing Time	Duty Hours	Spread-over
	A.M.	P.M.	H. M.	H. M.
1	4.43	12.57	7.41	8.14
2	4.50	12.50	7.30	8. 0
3	4.57	1.15	7.43	8.18
4	5. 5	1.23	7.42	8.18
5	5.12	1.13	7.30	8. 1
6	5.19	1.31	7.41	8.12
7	5.26	1.55	7.53	8.29
8	5.33	3.53	8.42	10.20
9	5.40	4.25	8.42	10.45
10	5.47	5. 8	8.42	11.21
11	7.58	7. 1	8. 0	11. 3
12	8.19	7. 8	7.54	10.49
13	11. 3	7.23	7.47	8.20
14	10.55	7.35	8. 5	8.40
15	11.21	7.47	7.49	8.26
16	11.37	8. 0	7.52	8.23
17	p.m. 12.35	10.10	7.47	9.35
18	1.59	10.49	8.12	8.50
19	3. 0	11. 6	7.30	8. 6
20	2.42	11. 8	7.49	8.26
21	2.50	11.18	7.51	8.28
22	3.20	11.54	7.56	8.34
Total	Duty	Hours	174.18	
Average	per	Duty	7.55	

SATURDAY				
Duty No.	Report Time	Finishing Time	Duty Hours	Spread-over
	A.M.	P.M.	H. M.	H. M.
1	4.43	12.48	7.30	8. 5
2	4.50	1.30	8. 8	8.40
3	4.59	1.36	8. 5	8.37
4	5. 5	1.42	8. 7	8.37
5	5.12	1.24	7.36	8.12
6	5.19	1.54	8. 5	8.35
7	5.26	2. 6	7.30	8.40
8	5.33	3.16	8. 0	9.43
9	5.37	3.38	8.10	10. 1
10	5.47	3.36	7.58	9.49
11	7. 8	3.54	8. 4	8.46
12	8. 5	5. 3	7.58	8.58
13	8.25	4.45	7.30	8.20
14	9.15	5.36	7.33	8.21
15	9.17	6. 9	7.41	8.52
16	11.38	8.17	8. 3	8.39
17	11.56	8.22	7.30	8.26
18	p.m. 12.33	9. 7	7.36	8.34
19	p.m. 12.26	10.36	8.12	10.10
20	2.11	10.49	7.30	8.38
21	3. 9	11.18	7.30	8. 9
22	3.17	11.18	7.30	8. 1
23	3.42	11.54	7.35	8.12
Total	Duty	Hours	179.21	
Average	per	Duty	7.48	

SUNDAY				
Duty No.	Report Time	Finishing Time	Duty Hours	Spread-over
	A.M.	P.M.	H. M.	H. M.
1	6.22	2.24	7.30	8. 2
2	6.38	2.41	7.30	8. 3
3	6.51	4.19	7.35	9.28
4	7. 3	3.16	7.36	8.13
5	8.47	4.51	7.30	8. 4
6	9.12	5.34	7.44	8.22
7	p.m. 1.22	9.39	7.30	8.17
8	2.25	10.30	7.30	8. 5
9	2.37	10.46	7.30	8. 9
10	3. 2	11.18	7.31	8.16
11	3.40	11.54	7.30	8.14
Total	Duty	Hours	82.56	
Average	per	Duty	7.32	

Duty Rota

Rota Week No.	Wednesday Duty No.	Wednesday Hours	Thursday Duty No.	Thursday Hours	Friday Duty No.	Friday Hours	Saturday Duty No.	Saturday Hours	Sunday Duty No.	Sunday Hours	Monday Duty No.	Monday Hours	Tuesday Duty No.	Tuesday Hours	Total Duty Hours Per Week
		H. M.		H. M.		H. M.		H. M.		H. M.		H. M.		H. M.	H. M.
1	1	7.41	1	7.41	1	7.41	6	8. 5	3	7.35	REST	DAY	14	8. 5	46.48
2	14	8. 5	14	8. 5	14	8. 5	15	7.41	9	7.30	19	7.30	REST	DAY	46.56
3	REST	DAY	19	7.30	19	7.30	20	7.30	6	7.44	8	8.42	8	8.42	47.38
4	8	8.42	REST	DAY	8	8.42	5	7.36	2	7.30	2	7.30	2	7.30	47.30
5	2	7.30	2	7.30	REST	DAY	10	7.58	11	7.30	22	7.56	22	7.56	46.20
6	22	7.56	22	7.56	22	7.56	21	7.30	REST	DAY	12	7.54	12	7.54	47. 6
7	12	7.54	12	7.54	12	7.54	14	7.33	REST	DAY	15	7.49	19	7.30	46.34
8	19	7.30	13	7.47	9	8.42	8	8. 0	REST	DAY	6	7.41	6	7.41	47.21
9	6	7.41	6	7.41	6	7.41	4	8. 7	REST	DAY	18	8.12	18	8.12	47.34
10	18	8.12	18	8.12	18	8.12	18	7.36	REST	DAY	5	7.30	5	7.30	47.12
11	5	7.30	5	7.30	5	7.30	3	8. 5	REST	DAY	21	7.51	21	7.51	46.17
12	21	7.51	21	7.51	21	7.51	19	8.12	REST	DAY	7	7.53	7	7.53	47.31
13	7	7.53	7	7.53	7	7.53	2	8. 8	10	7.31	REST	DAY	15	7.49	47. 7
14	15	7.49	15	7.49	15	7.49	16	8. 3	4	7.36	10	8.42	REST	DAY	47.48
15	REST	DAY	10	8.42	10	8.42	7	7.30	7	7.30	13	7.47	13	7.47	47.58
16	13	7.47	REST	DAY	13	7.47	17	7.30	5	7.30	9	8.42	9	8.42	47.58
17	9	8.42	9	8.42	REST	DAY	13	7.30	8	7.30	17	7.47	17	7.47	47.58
18	17	7.47	17	7.47	17	7.47	REST	DAY	1	7.30	3	7.43	3	7.43	46.17
19	3	7.43	3	7.43	3	7.43	9	8.10	REST	DAY	20	7.49	20	7.49	46.57
20	20	7.49	20	7.49	20	7.49	23	7.35	REST	DAY	14	8. 5	10	8.42	47.49
21	10	8.42	8	8.42	2	7.30	1	7.30	REST	DAY	4	7.42	4	7.42	47.48
22	4	7.42	4	7.42	4	7.42	12	7.58	REST	DAY	16	7.52	16	7.52	46.48
23	16	7.52	16	7.52	16	7.52	22	7.30	REST	DAY	11	8. 0	11	8. 0	47. 6
24	11	8. 0	11	8. 0	11	8. 0	11	8. 4	REST	DAY	1	7.41	1	7.41	47.26
											Total	Duty	Hours		1,133.47

PUBLIC SERVICE VEHICLE LICENCES AND REGULATIONS

PASSENGER TRANSPORT YEAR BOOK (1957)

P.S.V. LEGAL DIGEST

The following notes summarise some of the more important regulations and legal requirements governing the operation of passenger-carrying vehicles in Great Britain. The term "public service vehicle", it will be noticed, does not include trams and trolleybuses, which are subject to hackney carriage laws and local Acts. Only a general picture of the law's precise requirements is given, although these do not affect the basic effect of those quoted.

THE LICENSING SYSTEM

Under the Road Traffic Act, 1930, Traffic Commissioners were appointed to control the activities of passenger transport operators in specified Traffic Areas all over the country. There are now 11 of these areas, one covering the whole of Scotland and the other 10 the rest of England and Wales.

Construction and use regulations, conditions of fitness, and restrictions on driving time were items which were established by the 1930 and 1933 Acts. The Road Traffic Act of 1934 introduced driving tests as a condition of the issue of driving licenses, speed limits (30 m.p.h. for all p.s.v.'s), and amendments to the preceding regulations which experience revealed as necessary. Other amendments have been made from time to time, to meet changing conditions; in general, however, only the latest requirements are dealt with, except in some special cases, in the paragraphs that follow. The Road Traffic Act 1956 amended some of the regulations regarding traffic offences and the carriage of private coach parties.

CONSTRUCTION AND USE REGULATIONS

Under these regulations the following dimension and weight limitations are laid down.

Weight: Total laden weight of a four-wheeled (two-axle) p.s.v. must not exceed 12 tons; laden weight on one axle must not exceed 8 tons. In the case of a six-wheeled p.s.v. the one-axle limitation is the same, but the total laden weight must not exceed 14 tons. In the case of trolleybuses, an additional ½ ton may be added to the total laden weight of either four- or six-wheelers.

Height:

The maximum height permitted for p.s.v.'s is 15ft. In the case of trolleybuses, a height of 15ft. 10in. over the trolley base is permitted.

Length:

The maximum overall length of four- and six-wheeled single, half-deckers or double-deckers, is 30ft.

Width:

The maximum overall width of a p.s.v. must not exceed 8ft. Operation of 8ft wide vehicles under licence is restricted in the Metropolitan Traffic area to certain roads, while trolleybuses are restricted to 7ft. 6in. overall width except where special authority for the use of 8ft. wide trolleybuses is granted by the Ministry of Transport. Under Construction and Use Regulations, overall width excludes such items as exterior driving mirrors, and direction indicators which extend when operated; nothing else may extend more than 6in. beyond the outer edge of the outer rear tyre. Under conditions of fitness regulations, no part of a wheel or hub may extend more than 3½ in. beyond the outer surface of a fully inflated tyre.

Ground Clearance:

On all vehicles a minimum ground clearance of 10in. with the vehicle fully laden must be provided. Ground clearance under the rear platform of a double-decker must be a minimum of 10in. with the vehicle fully laden, but must not exceed 17in. when the vehicle is unladen. Conditions of fitness regulations provide that guard rails must be provided between the wheels on each side of the vehicle to within 9in. of the front wheels and to within 6in., of the rear wheels. These must be hinged and easily detachable.

Turning Circle:

All p.s.v.'s registered on or after June 1st, 1950, and with an overall length not exceeding 27ft., must be able to turn in a circle not over 60ft., or 66ft. if the overall length is over 27ft.

Rear Overhang:

The overhang of the body beyond the back axle must not exceed 7⁄24th of the actual maximum overall length, overhang being measured from the extreme rear of the vehicle to the centre line of the rear axle in two-axle vehicles, or to a point 4in. behind a line midway between the two rear axles in the case of a six-wheeler.

Dimensions (Interior):

In single-deckers, and on the lower deck of double-deckers, a minimum headroom of 5ft. 10in. must be provided, measured at the centre level of the gangway. This dimension is 5ft. 8in. in the case of the upper deck of double-deckers. In the case of vehicles seating under 15 passengers, the minimum headroom required is 5ft. 3in.; in school buses seating over 14, the minimum headroom required is 5ft. 6in.

Seats:

A space of at least 2ft. 2in. must be provided between rows of seats, measured from the back of one seat to the same point on the seat immediately behind or in front. In the case of facing seats, the distance between them may be reduced to a minimum of 1ft. 7in. A minimum of 1ft. 4in. width must be provided for each passenger on each seat. In the case of inward facing seats, a gangway width between the seats of at least 1ft. 9in. is required. Otherwise, the minimum gangway width is 1ft. from floor level up to 2ft. 6in. from the floor, and above that point a clear width of 1ft. 2in. (minimum) is required.

On double-deck vehicles, the rear platform must be open at least 3ft. along the length of the vehicle, and at least 1ft. 6in. along the back, except where an additional exit is provided on the nearside of the lower deck, in which case the open rear section is not required. Stairs in double-deckers must be at least 1ft. 9in. wide, and have a minimum tread of 9in. In single-deckers, the entrance must be at least 1ft. 9in. wide. On double-deckers, an emergency exit must be provided on the upper deck measuring at least 5ft. wide by 11ft. 6in. wide.

Mechanical Requirements:

Two independent braking systems, arranged in such a way that failure of any part (except a brake shoe, anchor pin or other fixed part) still leaves, on at least half the total number of wheels, braking adequate to stop the vehicle in a reasonable distance, under the most adverse conditions, are required on all vehicles. A parking brake, capable of preventing at least two of the wheels revolving, when the vehicle is unattended, is also required, and this may form one of the two independent means for braking specified. One of the two braking systems must be applied by direct mechanical means. In the case of vehicles with vacuum or air pressure servo braking systems, a warning device, visible to the driver, must be fitted to indicate failure or deficiency in the servo system. Transmission brakes are not permitted in p.s.v.'s, unless first registered before January 1st, 1933, or after January 1st, 1955. In the latter case, the brake must be independently hand operated and not foot operated, and must not have servo assistance of any kind whether pneumatic, hydraulic or electric. The brake must be attached direct to the final drive unit with no interposing universal joint, and the rear axle must be of the fully floating type. Braking systems depending upon the rotation of the engine are not permitted.

Fuel Tanks and Exhaust Pipes:

In petrol-engined vehicles, a shut-off cock must be provided between the tank and carburetter which is accessible from outside the vehicle and provided with visible markings indicating the "off" position. All fuel tank filling points must be outside the vehicle, and no tank may be fitted under a gangway within 2ft. of an entrance or exit. The exhaust pipe must be clear of, and shielded from any inflammable material, with its outlet on the offside at the rear of the vehicle, to obviate the possibility of fumes reaching the interior of the vehicle.

Lighting:

Adequate interior lighting, which must be kept on during hours of darkness, is required in all vehicles, and the staircase must be illuminated in double-deckers. Unless provided with a dipping device, headlamps must be permanently deflected downward, in such a way that a person standing 25ft. away is not dazzled at an eye level over 3ft. 6in. from the ground. If a lamp with a permanent deflected beam (such as a fog lamp) is located less than 2ft. from the ground, it may only be used in fog or falling snow. Except at traffic stops and when picking up or setting down passengers, headlamps must be switched off when the vehicle is stationary.

Two side lights are obligatory, and if the combined wattage of the lamps exceeds 7, a dipping mechanism or frosted glass lens is required.

Other requirements:

Steering arms must be polished but must not be painted or plated. Wheels must not foul the body or over-lock. Ball and socket joints, where used, must not be of the pendant type. In brake and steering connections, and in all parts which move or are subjected to vibration, lock nuts or split pins must be employed, and where bolts are located other than horizontally, the head must be uppermost.

A fire extinguisher of approved type is required on all p.s.v.'s and trolleybuses, while a pair of rubber gloves must form part of the equipment on all trolleybuses. On express carriage vehicles, a first aid kit, complete with approved contents, and a wheel lifting jack must be carried. A horn and a power-operated windscreen wiper are also required on all vehicles, although if the driver can see clearly by opening the windscreen, for example, the wiper is not essential. A rear-view mirror is legally required. A speedometer must be fitted to all p.s.v.'s.

Tilt Tests:

Before a certificate of fitness is issued for a p.s.v. it must pass a tilt or stability test. In the case of double-deckers, the vehicle must be capable of tilting without overturning to an angle of 28 degrees from the vertical with the upper deck loaded to the equivalent of 140lb. per passenger plus a conductor, if one is carried, and driver. Single-deckers first registered after October 1st, 1936, must be capable of tilting to 35 degrees without overturning under all conditions of loading.

DRIVERS AND CONDUCTORS

Licence conditions.

No one under 21 may be licenced as a p.s.v. driver, the minimum age for a conductor being 18. Licences are valid for three years. Drivers may drive for a total of 11 hours in a 24-hour period, from 2 a.m. In the course of this period no driver may drive for more than 5½ hours without at least 30 minutes' break for rest and refreshment. Unless he travels as a passenger, all the time a driver spends on a vehicle is counted as travelling time, although a driver may take his rest on the vehicle, if he has refreshment with him.

In addition, a driver must rest for 10 consecutive hours in any 24-hour period, calculated from the time when he started driving, or nine hours if, in the following 24 hours, he has 12 consecutive hours rest. A driver may work an 8½-hour shift, if during that time lay-over time is at least 45 minutes, or an 8-hour shift with at least 40 minutes lay-over. In the case of a split shift, totalling 8½ hours or less, the maximum driving period before rest may be raised to 6½ hours. In this case, at least 45 minutes lay-over time must be allowed, and 12 consecutive hours of rest provided in the 24 hours from the time when the driver began driving at the beginning of the first part of the shift.

Conductors are legally required to see that destination and fare indicators are properly displayed; they are also required to behave civilly, and, like drivers, must not smoke when passengers are on board a vehicle during a journey. They must ensure the safety of the passengers, and must not refuse to provide passengers with information on the route, fares, and destination. Conductors must not speak to the driver or distract his attention while the vehicle is moving, except to give instructions concerning stopping.

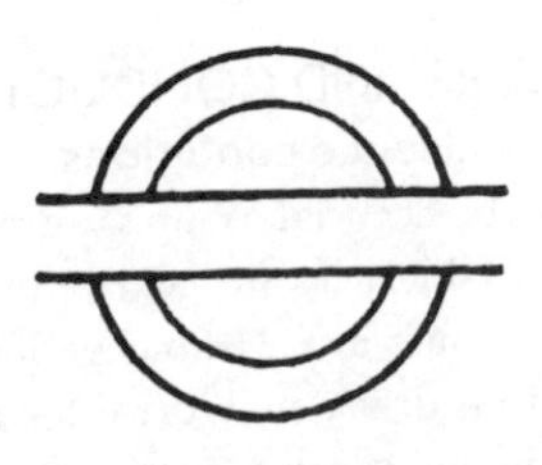

LOADING AND UNLOADING OF BUSES IN RELATION TO VEHICLE DESIGN

London Transport Executive, CT 204/128/002 (1955)

Some 12 to 15 per cent of the journey time of the average bus is spent in picking up and setting down passengers; any reduction in this stopping time would be of value in improving the speed and economy of bus operation. The time at the bus stop must depend to a large extent on the individual passengers boarding and alighting but their behaviour may be influenced by the vehicle itself, particularly in respect of the disposition of the entrance and exit (either separate or combined) and in the design of the platform, staircase and stops. The problem has, therefore, been closely investigated over the years by London Transport.

Experience has proved that for double-deck buses operating on in-town services a combined entrance and exit at either the front or the centre of the vehicle is unacceptable on grounds of passenger safety. The rear entrance (and exit) design has, therefore, been adopted by London Transport, and almost universally by other operators also. It seemed possible, however, that time spent in boarding and alighting might be reduced if passengers entered at the rear and left by an opening at the front of the bus. With such a design, it must still be possible for the conductor to regulate the number of boarding passengers; it becomes necessary, therefore, to place the front exit under the control of the driver and, in consequence, to provide it with a door. A trolleybus embodying a front exit with driver-controlled door was built by London Transport in 1937, and during the war years some 25 double-deck trolleybuses having a similar arrangement of separate entrance and exit were borrowed from Bournemouth. These buses were found to be unworkable on London routes due firstly to the general confusion caused by passengers who attempted to board at the front or leave at the rear, and secondly on account of loss of fares from short-journey passengers who could readily escape notice by the conductor. The front doors were, therefore, made inoperative and the rear opening used as a combined entrance and exit. It will be appreciated that a forward exit on double-deck buses necessitates an additional staircase at the front; this causes the loss of a minimum of eight seats. In addition, therefore, to the delays caused by misuse of the separate entrance and exit, a design of this sort would be a further source of congestion in that it would be necessary to provide an additional bus in every five or six (according to capacity) to give the same seating capacity as is obtained with vehicles of orthodox design.

An alternative arrangement, which reduces the confusion caused by an entrance and exit separated by the length of the vehicle, is to place them nearer together so that they can both be under the control of the conductor; it is, of course, necessary to provide doors. Considerable experience with vehicles of such design was obtained by London Transport during 1946 when experiments were being made with "Pay-as-you-board" buses, five of which were constructed by converting three standard double-deck buses and two trolleybuses. Two of the vehicles had a central entrance and exit while another two had an entrance and exit at the rear, twin-doors being fitted in each case. In the fifth vehicle, a bus, the entrance was at the extreme front and the exit some three feet away, doors being again provided. The "Pay-as-you-board" design involved a loss in capacity, this amounting to as much as six passenger seats in the rear entrance and exit bus. The two vehicles with central entrance and exit gave rise to such excessive delays in boarding and alighting as to necessitate their being withdrawn from service. The experiments were continued with the remaining three vehicles and clearly demonstrated that on many routes the "Pay-as-you-board" principle led to excessively long loading times, so much so that the vehicles were quite unable to maintain headways. At the same time it was also established that the doors in themselves caused an increase in the time spent in picking up and setting down passengers. It is relevant to add that experiments with a twin-door single deck trolleybus of the

"Pay-as-you-board" design were carried out by Glasgow Corporation during 1951. It is understood that there also it was found that the twin-door vehicle, whether worked on the "Pay-as-you-board" principle or in the normal manner so far as fare collection was concerned, was slower in operation on long heavy routes than the standard rear-entrance vehicles.

In view of London Transport's adverse experience with the various alternatives, the rear entrance design was retained for the RT type bus which was adopted in replacement of the pre-1939 fleet. Some years ago, however, a study was made of typical double-deck buses and trolleybuses in service, to discover whether the differences between them in respect of rear platform, staircase and steps, led to any measurable differences in the speeds of loading and unloading. The work was undertaken as an operational research project when consideration was being given to the design of a new double-deck bus, two prototypes of which (the RM) have since been constructed and are under test.

Four types of rear-entrance vehicle were selected for study, namely:

(a) the standard RT bus, which is 7 ft. 6 ins. wide;

(b) its 8 ft. wide counterpart, the RTW, which is similar except that the platform and gangways are respectively 6 inches and 4 inches wider;

(c) the standard 7 ft. 6 ins. wide trolleybus, whose platform is only very slightly smaller than that of the RT, and

(d the 8 ft. wide trolleybus which has a platform both 6 inches wider and 6 inches longer than the 7 ft. 6 ins. trolleybus, and moreover has a staircase with 9 steps, compared with 8 on the other three types, for the same total rise.

The differences between these four types of vehicles are admittedly not great, but they represent the variations which are possible within the limitation of not encroaching upon seating capacity.

Quantitative information on rates of boarding and alighting was obtained in a survey made at a number of bus stops during peak periods. So that the conditions under which the various types of vehicle were tested should be comparable, the stopping places selected were those where RT, RTW and/or trolleybus vehicles could be observed and a number of such places were used. Separate timings were made of boarding and alighting and of upper and lower deck flows. A total of 3,600 such timings was made and 38,000 passengers were counted; the number of passengers in each count varied from two or three to twenty-five or more but latecomers, who arrived at the bus after the main queue had boarded, were not counted. Furthermore, it had to be recognised that movement is frequently interrupted by the actions of passengers or conductors or by the conditions on the pavement, and that such delays might have little connection with the design of the vehicle; when such a delay occurred the observer made a note of the apparent cause. The results of the survey were subjected to statistical analysis.

Excluding, for the moment, those occasions when there appeared to the observer to be an interruption to the steady flow of passengers, there was no difference between the types of vehicle in the time taken for a given number of passengers to pass the edge of the platform on their way on to or off the bus. This time was proportional to the number of passengers and could be expressed as a rate, in terms of "seconds per passenger"; the rates of boarding and alighting for all four types of vehicle were:

Boarding the Lower Deck	1.7 seconds per passenger
Boarding the Upper Deck	1.9 seconds per passenger
Alighting from the Lower Deck	1.4 seconds per passenger
Alighting from the Upper Deck	1.6 seconds per passenger

This result, that the differences between vehicle types are negligible, can be better understood if the actions of a stream of passengers mounting a step in succession are considered. The speed of the individual depends upon his agility and on the height of the step to be mounted, and a person will not ordinarily move so close as to fall foul of the feet of the person in front. It follows that the rate of boarding and alighting is always subject to these human limitations.

When account was taken of all the observations, including any delays which occurred, the average effect was to increase the boarding times by one tenth of a second per passenger and the alighting time by about half this. Again, there was no significant difference between the vehicle types.

Some interest attaches to the types of delay which were seen to occur even though, as was shown, their overall effect on loading and unloading time was extremely small. Boarding passengers were delayed on 30 per cent of occasions, but alighting passengers were affected less often. Most of these delays were uncaused by the passengers themselves and occurred irrespective of the type of vehicle. Only in the case of these few delays which the conductor caused was there any difference between the vehicle types; it appeared that in the wider 8 ft. buses and trolleybuses the conductor was able to collect the fares more quickly, for he was seen to be on the platform at the stop more often on these vehicles and was less often observed to be collecting the fares of passengers as they alighted. It was also demonstrated that, if the conductor stands with his back against the staircase, he does not hinder the flow of passengers at all.

It was concluded that, based upon the proportions of the rear platform type of entrance in use by London Transport, there is little possibility of reducing the time which buses must spending picking up and setting down passengers. In the light of this, the RM 64-seater bus was designed to embody the entrance typified by the 8 ft. wide RTW bus which had been shown to contribute to a reduction in delays caused by the conductor in collecting fares from passengers about to alight, and incidentally also, to facilitate the collection of fares at all times.

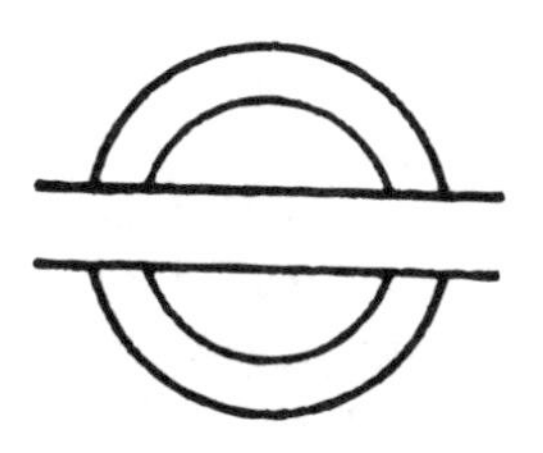

LONDON TRANSPORT'S NEW DOUBLE-DECK BUS

Technical Information (1954)

London Transport's road vehicle engineers, led by Mr. A.A.M. Durrant, C.B.E., the Chief Mechanical Engineer for the Road Services, have evolved a new type of double-deck bus to replace the existing 70-seater three-axled trolleybuses. They set themselves the task of providing a two-axle vehicle, of all-metal construction, capable of carrying 64 seated passengers, within a loaded weight no greater than that of the present 56-seater RT bus.

A prototype of the new vehicle, further developed and constructed in association with A.E.C. Ltd, and Park Royal Vehicles Ltd., will be on show at the Commercial Vehicle Exhibition. Incorporating many advanced features of double-deck bus design, it is particularly suited to cope with severe conditions of city working, with long life and economy in operation and maintenance.

DESIGN

The vehicle has been designed for maximum seating capacity, minimum weight, ease of control and ease of servicing and overhaul, and is of monocoque construction. The 64-seater bus is 27' 0" long, 8' 0" wide and has a wheelbase of 16' 9".

The estimated laden weight is 11 tons, to achieve which general savings in weight in both body structure and mechanical units have been necessary. They have been effected in the body structure by the use of light alloys, fibreglass and other weight-saving materials, with the result that the estimated unladen kerb weight is 6 tons 17 cwts 2 qrs., inclusive of fuel, oil, water, etc. No conventional chassis frame is employed, the body structure serving as the main load-carrying unit, with small sub-frames to mount the mechnical units at front and rear, these being so arranged as to be easily removable for overhaul.

Independent front suspension and a patented form of coil spring rear suspension are used to give a wide roll centre which promotes vehicle stability coupled with much improved riding characteristics. A special design of engine mounting prevents the transmission of engine vibration to the body structure.

In the interests of driving efficiency the pre-selector pedal has been eliminated, direct engagement of gears being by electro-hydraulic valves controlled by a column-mounted gear shift lever. The hand-brake lever is positioned to the left of the driving position to facilitate entry to the cab, and much improved ventilation, heating and demisting is provided.

Special features of the vehicle design are covered by the following patents:

704562	701106	701616
712326	700392	704363

and provisional patents:

12346/53	18139/63	14578/54

BODY STRUCTURE

MAIN STRUCTURE

The four-bay vehicle structure consists of an extremely rigid box formed by the underframe, sides, roof and front and rear bulkheads, and is fabricated from high-duty aluminium alloy throughout. The front bulkhead carries the driver's cab and front nearside units – wing, bonnet, front cowling etc., – while the rear platform structure, staircase, etc., are suspended from the upper saloon. Attention has been paid to the need for ease of repair and replacement of front and rear and body parts, and to the removal of running units for overhaul and maintenance purposes, a necessary feature to conform with the routine maintenance system in force in London.

The underframe consists of rigid cross-members of great depth each completely lubricated from high-duty aluminium alloy, in the form of a 'I' beam of great strength. Bolted to the end of each are the lower saloon side pillars, the connection being made with angle member between the 'H'-section pillar and the cross-member. The lower saloon body side is made up of the 'H'-section extruded alloy pillars with sheet stress panels from waist to skirt solid-riveted to the inside flange of the pillar and bolted between the crossbearer and pillar. The waist rail and cant rail are a simple channel riveted to the pillars in bay lengths providing anchorage for the panelling and window pans. Exterior panelling of aluminium sheet is butt-jointed and blind riveted to the framing without vertical cover strips, the stress panelling being fitted internally to minimise replacement difficulties in the event of accident damage.

Floor bearers for the intermediate roof are of similar form to the main cross-members though not so deep, and extend from pillar to pillar, and form the anchorage of the upper saloon pillars, which are again of extruded alloy in 'H' form, but of lighter section than those in the lower deck. The stress panels of the upper saloon are fitted externally, not being subject to much damage, also butt-jointed without vertical cover strips, and an interior trim panel of sheet aluminum is solid riveted to the framing. The waist and cant rail are again of simple channel section, and a similar member is fitted at intermediate floor level for securing the base of the upper saloon stress panel and the panel over the lower saloon windows.

The upper roof structure is of square-section alloy tube, with riveted overlapped exterior panelling in alloy sheet, in bay lengths from front to rear, and with aluminium sheet front and rear domes. The floors and ceilings are made entirely from alloy sheeting; in corrugated form this performs the load-carrying functions and in sheet form provides ceilings, floor coverings, and, in the case of the lower deck floor, an easily cleaned underside of the body. On both decks the ceiling panels extend from cant rail to cant rail in bay lengths, the pillar pitch being 4' 1⅓" centres. The divisions between sections of sheet flooring occur at the longitudinals either side of the gangway. An interesting feature of the upper deck floor is that the sheeting is laid in three flats instead of

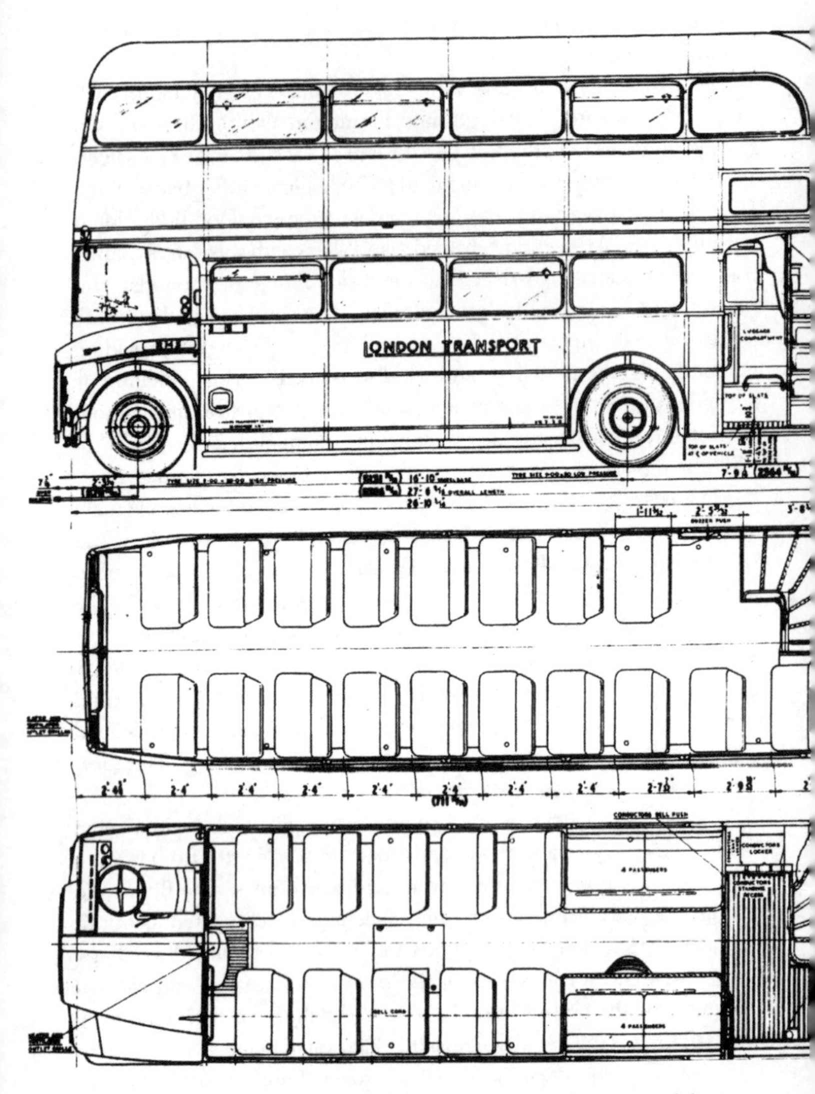

Plan and overhead views showing the profile and seating arrangements of the upper and lower saloons of the 64-seater Routemaster

orthodox radius. Floor cover panels of chequered aluminium plate are fitted to both decks.

The rear wheelboxes and footstools are fabricated in sheet alloy and are of exceedingly rigid construction, since they form beams for the support of the rear suspension unit, and house the two rear coil springs and shock absorbers. These are built into the rear bulkhead which is in alloy sheet extending up to and tied in with the intermediate floor. The rear platform framing is suspended from the upper saloon rear and the platform floor is alloy framed and covered with alloy sheet, suitably stiffened. The rear end framing, extending round the rear quarter and up to cant level, is designed to be mostly removable in the event of damage, and to facilitate working to the rear end, the staircase – similar in shape to existing London vehicles – is split at the fourth tread and the lower portion is easily removable.

The front bulkhead, having a continuous channel member from side to side above the flywheel arch, has a skin of aluminium alloy on the forward face to which are riveted the channels and angles forming the bulkhead proper. Two robust buttresses are built onto the front face of the bulkhead on each side of the flywheel arch to form the anchorage for the vertically positioned front sub-frame attachment bolts, and are so designed as to spread the load evenly onto the bulkhead. The rear anchorages of the front sub-frame are built in to the ends of the front main cross-bearer and the bodyside, to carry the horizontally disposed attachment bolts, and additional alloy sheet trussing extends forward to the bulkhead and back to the second bearer, to spread the load over a larger area.

JACKING POINTS

For lifting the vehicle during removal of the running units, lifting and jacking points are provided adjacent to front and rear bulkheads. The front lifting points are incorporated in the driver's recessed step and a similar step in the nearside with locating pegs positioned beneath the skirt to support the body on jacks, similar pegs being fitted adjacent to the rear bulkhead with appropriate lifting recesses.

CAB, BONNET, ETC

The driver's cab, in which special attention has been given to the siting and dispositon of all controls, is generally similar to the current London vehicles and is cantilevered off the bulkhead, being removable in sections to facilitate repair and replacement. To the nearside of the cab, the fibreglass bonnet top is hinged to the front bulkhead, and is of spring-balanced type. The enveloping type of front nearside wing is suspended from the bulkhead on flexible bushes, having the radiator header tank and filler housed within, also mounted on the bulkhead. Fibreglass is used for the wing valances. The frontal grille and front end shaped panelling, in sheet aluminium, carries the usual lamp equipment, and has a small hinged panel for access to the oil filter, dipstick and fuel cock. The centre front panel and a section of the nearside wing are removable for access to the engine.

The cab is fitted with a heater and demister, both of which supply cold or warmed fresh air, with a safety switching to cut the fan if the fresh air control is closed, thus preventing re-circulation of already heated air within the enclosed space of the cab. The top and bottom cab screens are of winder operated type similar to those used in current bodies.

PLATFORM & FLOORING

Beneath the stairs there is sufficient space for the conductor to stand comfortably, leaving ample room for unobstructed passenger flow. The fare-table forms the door to the conductor's locker at shoulder height beneath the stairs, luggage space also being provided on the battery compartment.

The gangway floor and platform are covered with a rubber/cork composition; bevelled slats and tiles of the same material are cemented down between and beneath the seats. The spaces between the slats facilitate floor cleaning.

WINDOWS ETC.

The main saloon windows are inside rubber glazed in alloy pans having polished interior rims, beneath which the flat inside finishers are inserted.

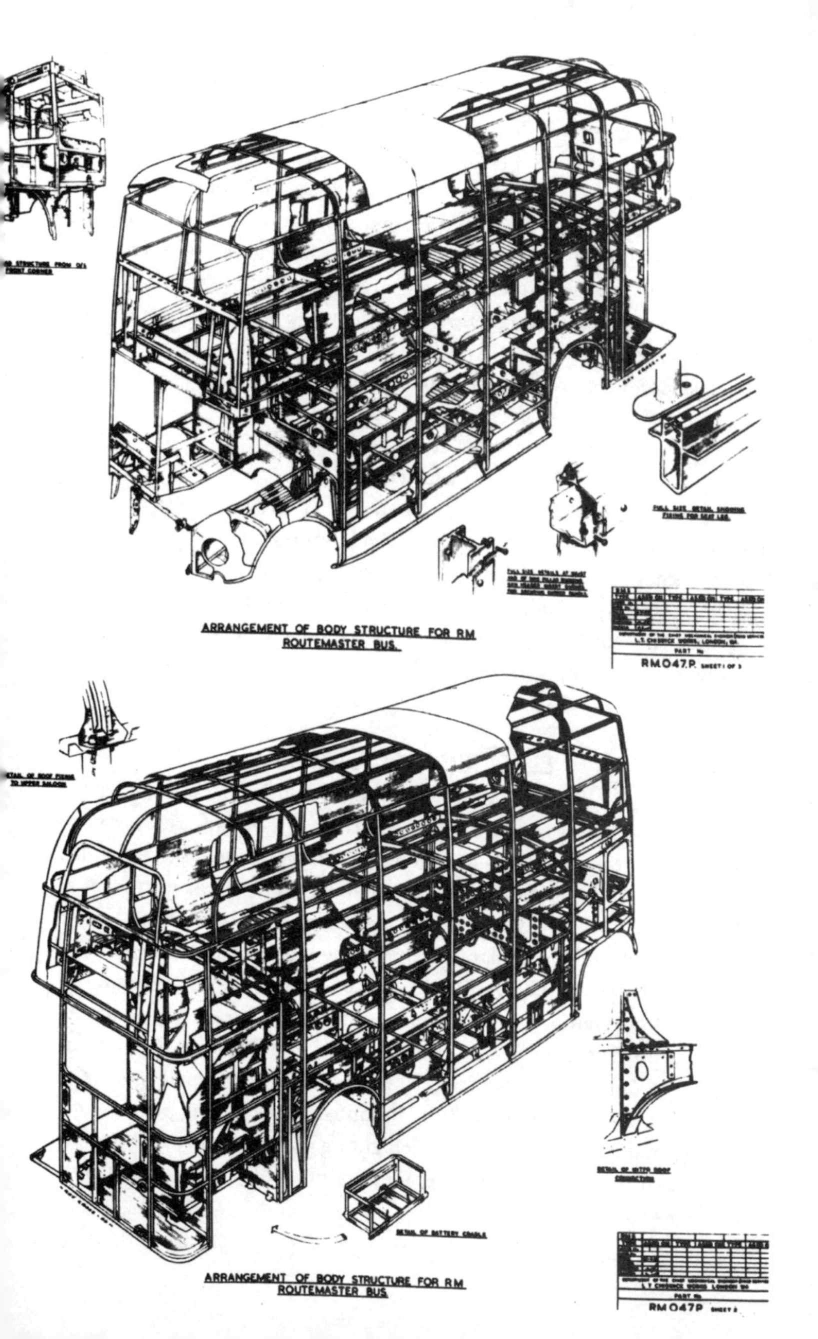
ARRANGEMENT OF BODY STRUCTURE FOR RM
ROUTEMASTER BUS.
PART No
RM.O47.P.
ARRANGEMENT OF BODY STRUCTURE FOR RM
ROUTEMASTER BUS
RM O47P

Four opening side windows in the lower saloon and six in the upper are of alloy framed high-level winder type with no bottom rail to the moving portion. These are so designed as to facilitate cleaning. The forward facing opening windows are provided with a locking mechanism to prevent opening in cold weather. Two of the fixed glasses in each saloon are of breakable type for emergency use, whilst an alloy frame of pressed sections with curved toughened glass forms the rear emergency exit in the upper deck. Two slot-type adjustable intake vents are provided in each saloon front framing, controlled by the conductor.

SEATING

The seating capacity of 64 is disposed so that 28 seats are in the lower saloon and 36 in the upper, on London Transport service type tubular seat frames. The squab backs are fabricated from fibreglass, and the cushion and squab fillings, in the interests of lightness, are of formed plastic. The seat and squab trimming is in moquette with hide ends, with leathercloth trim in the squab back.

ELECTRICAL EQUIPMENT

The batteries – four six-volt units – are carried in a cradle under the stairs. This cradle is in light alloy and permits removal of batteries from outside, but topping-up is carried out via a hinged flap under the stairs. Winking direction indicators of arrow form are fitted at cant level at the front of the body hinged to prevent accidental damage, and these are electrically linked to arrow lamps in the rear panels at waist level.

Centrally below the waist in the rear end is the illuminated number plate and stop lamp assembly, while combined red reflectors and rear lamps are fitted at each side, the nearside unit forming the bottom bracket of the rear end handrail. The saloon lamps, of open type, have special fittings allowing each to be mounted to the ceiling panels from the saloon side, since no detachable lighting cover panels are provided. In the interests of weight saving, aluminium cables and conduits are largely used.

DESTINATION INDICATORS ETC.

Destination indicators are provided at front, rear and over the platform on the nearside, all of lightweight construction and operable from within. An illuminated route number box is also built in above the nearside front bulkhead window.

LIVERY AND TRIM

Externally the traditional livery of red with cream band remains, but the interior colour scheme is a departure from current practice. The seat trimming is a patterned moquette toning well with the interior finishing colour of Damask Red and ceiling panels of Sung Yellow. The squab backs are trimmed in Chinese Green leathercloth. A polished alloy moulding separates the two colours, and has a white plastic insert in the centre. Platform and staircase stanchions and handrails together with their bracket and fittings are of stainless steel, while those fitted in both saloons are of polished alloy. The layout of these stanchions etc., follows normal practice.

MECHANICAL UNITS

FRONT SUB-FRAME

The engine, steering and front suspension are carried on a sub-frame which consists mainly of two pressed channel-section longitudinal members. They extend forward from the front bulkhead and are attached at four points, two at No. 2 cross bearer and two at buttresses built on to the front bulkhead. In plan the members converge towards the front, being anchored to the main body sides at No. 2 cross bearer and reduced to normal chassis width at the front.

The longitudinals are joined by two cross-members; a substantial fabricated box-section member under the centre of the engine carries the main engine mountings, and the mountings of the independent front suspension units, whilst a channel-section member joins the front ends of the longitudinals and supports the front of the engine. At each of the four body attachement points, a large pin or bolt forms the main attachment, with a shallow double conical packing interposed in seatings between the two connected assemblies for location purposes. The two pins at the front bulkhead are carried vertically, while those at the rear are horizontal.

In order to remove the front running unit assembly, or 'horse', the propellor shaft, controls, fuel and brake lines, etc. are disconnected and the pins of the front attachment points are removed. The main vehicle structure is then lifted at the front running gear unit hinges down about the rear attachment points until the steering column has cleared the cab floor. The two rear attachment points are then disconnected and the running unit wheeled forward on the two front wheels.

ENGINE

The engine is the well-known and proven A.E.C. 9.6 litre direct-injection unit developing 125 b.h.p. at 1,800 r.p.m. and because of the absence of a conventional frame and leaf springs can be mounted offset towards the left-hand side. The engine is slightly modified to suit the special requirements of the vehicle but is basically the same as the unit used in existing London Transport vehicles.

The main engine mounting is approximately at the centre of the engine and consists of two rubber sandwich units positioned to form a vee about the longitudinal axis of the engine and attached to facings on the crankcase bottom half. A third mounting point is in the form of a large circular rubber unit on the front of the cylinderblock and carried at the front main member, following current A.E.C. practice.

The gear ratings are:

1st speed	4.28:1
2nd speed	2.43:1
3rd speed	1.59:1
4th speed	1:1
Reverse	5.97:1

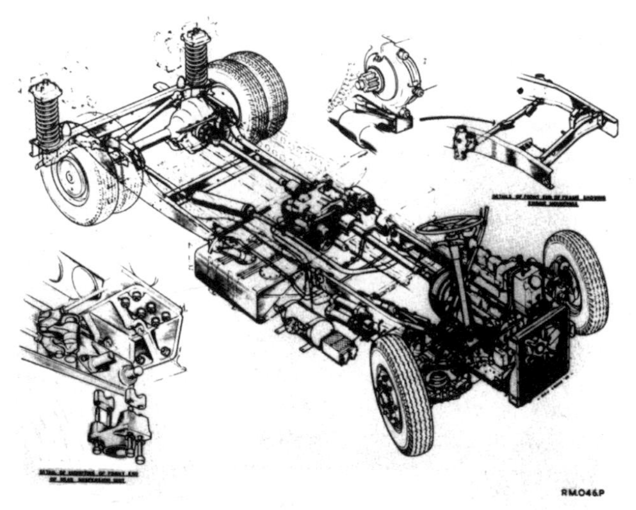

REAR AXLE

The rear axle reduction is by spiral bevel gears and has fully floating axle shafts. The drive unit is offset towards the left hand and the the ratio is 5.22:1.

The axle casing is a forged steel banjo-shaped member with the tube holes bored from the solid. The crown wheel is mounted on the differential casings which are carried on taper roller bearings in a detachable housing whilst the pinion is straddle mounted with opposed taper roller bearings and a parallel roller bearing.

The hubs are mounted on the parallel roller bearings separated by distance rings and clamped by large nuts on the axle casing. Lip type seals are provided to retain the lubricant.

REAR SUSPENSION

The main members of this rear suspension are two spectacle radius arms of pressed channel section. They are pivoted at their front and on rubber bushes from brackets adjacent to the third main body bearer. The rear axle casing passes through the 'eyes' of the members and is attached to them by two inclined sandwich rubber mountings on each side. The radius arms extend backward and are bolted to an 'I'-section member of two channels back to back which extends across almost the width of the vehicle behind the rear axle, and reacts at its outer ends against the rear coil springs which are housed in the wheelboxes. Telescopic direct-noting hydraulic dampers are enclosed within the springs and progressive rubber bump units are provided to prevent sudden shock loads from being transmitted to the main structure. A further light channel member ties the two radius arms together in front of the axle. Lifting of one wheel only is accommodated by the rubber bush anchorage and by allowing the suspension members to weave. Lateral location is by a transverse radius rod extending from a bracket on the right-hand side of the axle casing to the left-hand side of the main body structure.

The rear suspension can be removed as a unit after disconnecting the propeller shaft, hand brake rod, brake pipot, front pivot pins, transverse rod and spring and hydraulic damper attachments.

FRONT SUSPENSION

Independent front suspension is used with unequal length wishbones and coil springs. The wishbone units are each pivoted to the main front cross-member (which also carries the engine mounting) and the swivel pin bosses by conical rubber bush units.

Conventional swival pins are fitted in the bosses carried by the suspension wishbones, and the hub assembly using bigger roller bearings follows current A.E.C. practice.

The coil springs are fitted between the lower wishbones and the top of the cross-member with direct-acting telescopic hydraulic dampers fitted inside the springs. The spring complete, with damper unit, can be removed from underneath by unscrewing eight bolts.

STEERING

Steering is by an A.E.C. worm and nut unit mounted on the front sub-frame so that the drop-arm moves in a transverse plane. The drop-arm is connected by a steering rod to a similar slave arm on the opposite side of the sub-frame. Short rods connect the steering swivels to the drop-arm on slave arm respectively.

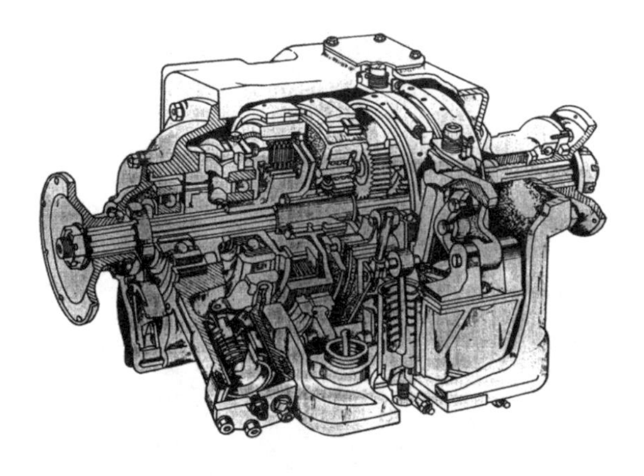

A.E.C. D182 direct selection epicyclic gearbox

BRAKES

The continuous flow hydraulic foot-brake system operates on all four wheels and the mechanical hand-brake on the rear wheels only.

All four brake drums are 15" in diameter with conventional landing and trailing shoes operated by 'S'-shaped arms, which in conjunction with worm and worm wheel type slack adjusters allow the linings to go throughout their lifetime without the necessity of introducing braking discs.

Hydraulic pressure is supplied by a pump mounted on the front of the gearbox and two bag-type accumulators are fitted on the right-hand side of the vehicle. The oil container is on the right-hand side with the filler accessible through the valves. The feed valve is a duplex unit to avoid complete loss of braking in the event of a pipe failure and the operating cylinders work directly on to the brake camshaft levers.

The hand-brake lever fitted on the driver's left-hand side is mechanically connected to the rear brakes by pull rods through ball crank levers without a cross shaft.

FUEL TANKS

The 25-gallon fuel tank is on the left-hand side and has a filler neck to suit the L.T. E. automatic shut-off re-fuelling arrangement.

TYRE EQUIPMENT

9.00-20 12-ply rating single front and twin 10-ply rear tyres are fitted.

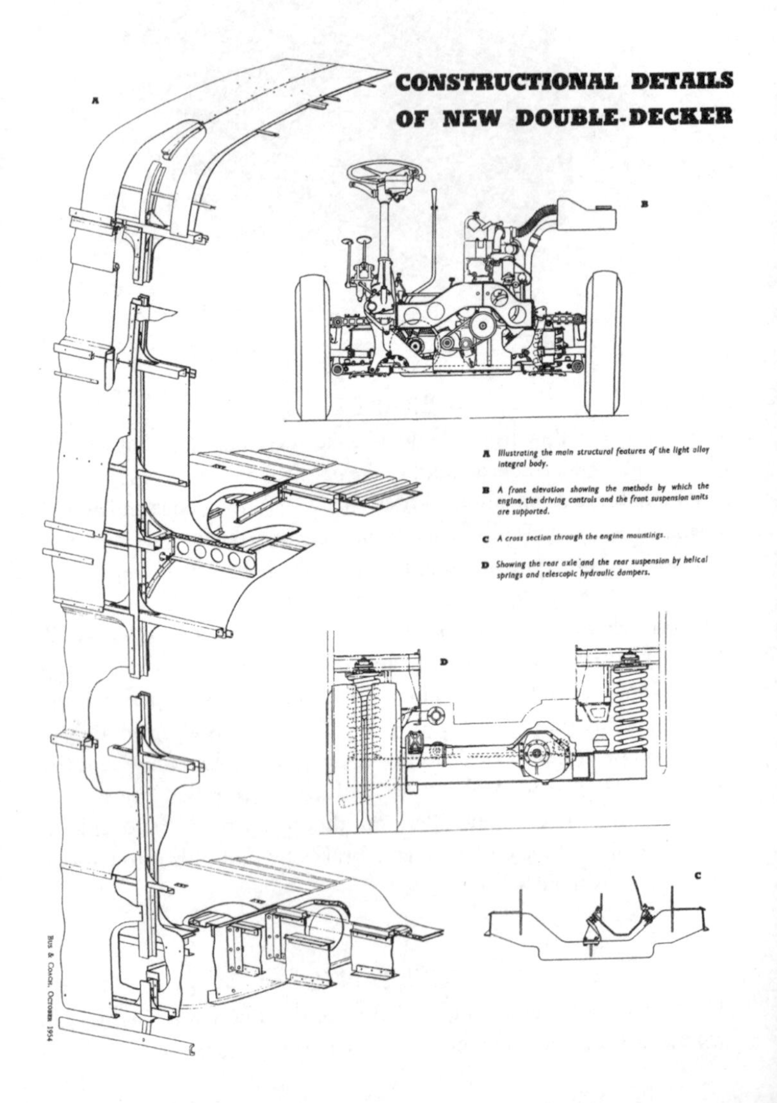

CONSTRUCTIONAL DETAILS OF NEW DOUBLE-DECKER

A *Illustrating the main structural features of the light alloy integral body.*

B *A front elevation showing the methods by which the engine, the driving controls and the front suspension units are supported.*

C *A cross section through the engine mountings.*

D *Showing the rear axle and the rear suspension by helical springs and telescopic hydraulic dampers.*

Bus & Coach, October 1954

WEST END SEES LONDON'S NEW 64-SEATER

'Evening News', January 31, 1956

FIRST BUS GOES INTO SERVICE NEXT WEEK

London's "bus of the future", the 64-seater Routemaster, appeared for the first time to-day when a special party toured the West End at the invitation of London Transport.

The first of the new buses will be put into service on route 2 (Golders Green–Crystal Palace) on Wednesday of next week, but the main fleet will not be in operation until the replacement of trolleybuses in 1959.

Mr A. M. Durrant, chief mechanical engineer of the L.T.E. road services, describes the Routemaster as "the most up-to-date public transport vehicle in the world".

It has no chassis, is six inches wider and one foot longer than the standard bus, which it will eventually replace, and seats more passengers.

Additional comfort for passengers is provided by the coil springs on the front and rear wheels – the first bus in the world to have "private car suspension".

Interior decoration has been brightened up and Mr J. B. Burnell, operating manager of the Central Road Services, told me:

"Our next step will be to provide interior heating to both lower and upper decks".

Mr J. B. Burnell added: "We shall begin replacing the trolleybus service with the new Routemaster in three years' time. I estimate that we shall need between 1,600 and 1,700 of the new buses at an approximate cost of £8,000,000.

To-day's bus caused great interest among waiting passengers in the sleet-swept streets of the West End.

Driver Edward J. Uwins, of Reigate, told me: "This is a piece of cake to handle compared with the present buses."

NEW LONDON BUS GIVES MORE ROOM

'The Star', January 31, 1956

Prototypes of a new 64 passenger bus – longer and wider but lighter than any on the roads – will go into service for the first time in London tomorrow week.

The new bus, known as the Routemaster, or RM1, is 27ft long and 8ft wide – that is, a foot longer and six inches wider than buses now in service. Yet it weighs only 11 tons fully loaded – 3 cwt lighter than standard 56-seater buses.

Londoners saw the bus for the first time today when it took a special party on a tour round the West End.

In difficult traffic conditions, with wet, greasy roads, RM1 gave an impressive performance.

"A first class job – the boys will like this", said it driver, Mr Edward J Uwins, of Reigate. The Routemaster is a lightweight among buses because it has been built throughout in aluminium alloy.

From the passenger's point of view the Routemaster has several advantages, in particular a wider gangway. The interior colour scheme is damask red, and bright yellow. There are drop windows and a large ventilator grid which can be used as an electric heater in winter.

Nor did the designers forget the conductor. He has been given a small alcove on his platform where he can stand to give passengers a clearer way when boarding and alighting.

The bus will go into service next Wednesday on Route 2 between Golders Green and Crystal Palace and later, on Route 1, Willesden to Lewisham, and Route 60, Colindale to Old Ford.

Three other prototypes are being built and quantity production will start in about three years' time. London Transport's aim is to replace the whole of its fleet.

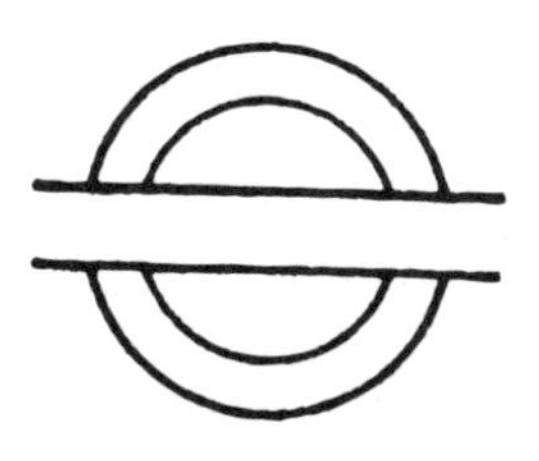

LONDON'S "BUS OF THE FUTURE" GOES INTO SERVICE – THE "ROUTEMASTER" TO BE TRIED OUT ON ROUTE 2 – WILL GIVE LONDONERS SMOOTHER RIDE

LONDON TRANSPORT PRESS RELEASE, G.P.N. 358 (1956)

The first prototype of London's "bus of the future", the 64-seater "Routemaster", goes into public service on route 2 between Golders Green and Crystal Palace on Wednesday, February 8, London Transport announce.

The new bus, which is of revolutionary design, will be given a thorough try-out in actual passenger service before it is produced in quantity in about three years' time to begin the replacement of London's trolleybuses as they become worn out.

The "Routemaster" prototype will operate from Cricklewood garage. After operating on route 2 it will be switched to route 1 (Willesden–Lewisham) and route 60 (Colindale–Old Ford). It will remain in public service for several months.

The bus was described today by Mr. A. A .M. Durrant, C.B.E., London Transport's Chief Mechanical Engineer (Road Services), as the most up-to-date vehicle of its kind in the world. It has been developed and constructed by London Transport engineers led by Mr. Durrant in association with A.E.C. Limited and Park Royal Vehicles Limited. Mr Durrant said:

"The 'Routemaster' is the London bus of the future. It will seat 64 passengers, 8 more than the present London double-decker diesel bus, the RT. It is also six inches wider and one foot longer than the standard RT, which will give more room in the bus. The 'Routemaster' prototype, before being out into passenger service, has been subjected to most strenuous testing over all sorts of extreme conditions at the vehicle proving grounds of the Motor Industry Research Association at Nuneaton where special tests were also conducted to measure the stresses in all parts of the vehicle's structure. After that the 'Routemaster' was subjected to 6,000 miles of most severe running on the Ministry of Supply's fighting vehicle proving ground at Chobham in Surrey, so that we are satisfied that fundamentally the vehicle is sound and has a fully adequate factor of safety. One of the tests the 'Routemaster' underwent at Chobham was to be put into a full lock skid while being driven at 30 m.p.h. This is a very critical test for any vehicle, particularly so with a double-decker bus, and the 'Routemaster' came through with flying colours and not the slightest risk of overturning. This is very striking evidence of the stability and road safety of the bus.

The 'Routemaster' is a light-weight job built throughout in aluminium alloy. The body is revolutionary. It has no chassis in the accepted sense. It is built like a very strong and rigid box; the wheels and mechanical units carried on small frames are attached direct to the 'box'. This new type of vehicle building saves weight, simplifies maintenance, and reduces wear and tear.

We have gone all out to save weight on the new bus – consistent with strength and comfort – because saving weight means a big fuel economy and helps us to keep our costs down. Apart from the basic material of light-weight aluminium alloy, we have saved further weight by using glass fibre for the wings, bonnet top, and seat backs, and filling the seat cushions with light-weight plastic foam. The result of all this is that the 'Routemaster', even though it carries 8 more passengers, will actually be lighter when fully laden than the present London double-decker bus.

It will be extremely quiet in running, and riding in it will be smoother than anything London has known before. The bus has 'private car type' springing with independent front-wheel coil-spring suspension and a new type of coil-sprung suspension for the rear wheels. Other features of the bus which we hope passengers will like are the interior colour scheme – damask red with bright yellow ceiling – drop windows, which give a better view, and a special recess under the stairs where the conductor can stand, thus giving passengers a clearer way when they board and alight. The extra six inches width of this bus will go on the gangways which will help both passengers and conductor in getting about the vehicle.

We have made the bus unique in its ease of driving control, which is most necessary when you consider the heavy conditions of traffic in London and the ever growing congestion. The 'Routemaster' will be as easy to drive as a modern car. The gear change is by a lever on the steering wheel which operates electro-hydraulic valves. We have done away with the gear change pedal so that the driver now has only two pedals to use, the accelerator and the brake. We are also fitting direction indicators of a special design."

The drivers from Cricklewood garage who will take this bus into passenger service on February 8 have been receiving training so that they can familiarise themselves with the new two-pedal control and its general handling. A second prototype 'Routemaster' has also been built and will soon go into public service so that London Transport's engineers can in the coming months see how these vehicles stand up to the stresses and strains of London passenger conditions before production of the final version is begun.

The "Routemaster" will also be used when the time comes to replace London's present RT type double-decker buses which, of course, are much younger than the trolleybuses and have many more years of life ahead of them.

LONDON TRANSPORT EXECUTIVE OPERATING DEPARTMENT (CENTRAL ROAD SERVICES) N.W. DIVISION

FROM:
DIVISIONAL SUPERINTENDENT,
N.W. DIVISION, DOLLIS HILL. 4th February, 1956

THE ROUTEMASTER – PROGRAMME OF OPERATION

I attach hereto details of the timetable operation for the Routemaster (R.M.1), the prototype A.E.C. 64-seat 8 foot wide vehicle.

Until further notice R.M.1 will be allocated to Cricklewood Garage and work on Route 2 as follows:–

Days of Operation	Date Commencing	Running No.	Period of Operation
Monday to Friday	Wednesday Feb. 8th	W.16	6.53 am to 9.29 pm
Saturday	Saturday Feb. 11th	W.9	8.25 am to 10.47 pm
Sunday	Sunday Feb 12th	W.1	7.26 am to 10.44 pm

It is important to confirm on each day that the bus is in fact running to these times.

LONDON TRANSPORT EXECUTIVE
THE ROUTEMASTER – PROGRAMME OF OPERATION
MONDAY TO FRIDAY – COMMENCING 8TH FEB. 1956.
RUNNING NUMBER W.16

CRICKLEWOOD GARAGE	6.53					
GOLDERS GREEN	–	9.44	12.38	3.30	6.33	9.16
CHILDS HILL	7.02	9.48	12.42	3.34	6.37	9.20
SWISS COTTAGE	7.10	9.56	12.50	3.42	6.45	–
BAKER STREET STN.	7.18	10.04	12.58	3.50	6.53	–
MARBLE ARCH	7.23	10.11	1.05	3.57	6.58	–
HYDE PARK CORNER	7.28	10.18	1.12	4.04	7.03	–
VICTORIA CLOCK TOWER	7.33	10.24	1.18	4.10	7.08	–
BRIXTON STATION	7.48	10.39	1.33	4.25	7.23	–
WEST NORWOOD	8.01	10.52	1.46	4.38	7.36	–
CRYSTAL PALACE	8.13	11.05	1.59	4.51	7.48	–

CRICKLEWOOD GARAGE						9.29
CRYSTAL PALACE	8.20	11.14	2.06	5.01	8.00	
WEST NORWOOD	8.31	11.26	2.18	5.13	8.11	
BRIXTON STATION	8.44	11.39	2.31	5.26	8.24	
VICTORIA CLOCK TOWER	8.59	11.54	2.46	5.41	8.39	
HYDE PARK CORNER	9.04	12.00	2.52	5.47	8.44	

MARBLE ARCH	9.11	12.07	2.59	5.54	8.49
BAKER STREET STN.	9.18	12.14	3.06	6.01	8.54
SWISS COTTAGE	9.26	12.22	3.14	6.09	9.02
GOLDERS GREEN	9.38	12.34	3.26	6.21	9.14

LONDON TRANSPORT EXECUTIVE
THE ROUTEMASTER – PROGRAMME OF OPERATION
SATURDAY – COMMENCING 11TH FEB. 1956
RUNNING NUMBER W.9

GOLDERS GREEN		8.40	11.34	2.23	5.12	7.54	10.34
CHILDS HILL		8.44	11.38	2.27	5.16	7.58	10.38
SWISS COTTAGE		8.53	11.47	2.36	5.25	8.07	–
BAKER STREET STN.		9.01	11.55	2.44	5.33	8.15	–
MARBLE ARCH		9.07	12.01	2.50	5.38	8.20	–
HYDE PARK CORNER		9.13	12.07	2.56	5.43	8.25	–
VICTORIA CLOCK TOWER		9.19	12.13	3.02	5.48	8.30	–
BRIXTON STATION		9.34	12.28	3.17	6.03	8.45	–
WEST NORWOOD		9.46	12.40	3.29	6.15	8.57	–
CRYSTAL PALACE		9.59	12.53	3.42	6.28	9.10	–
CRICKLEWOOD GARAGE	8.25						10.47
CRYSTAL PALACE	–	10.06	1.01	3.50	6.35	9.17	
WEST NORWOOD	–	10.18	1.13	4.02	6.47	9.29	
BRIXTON STATION	–	10.30	1.25	4.14	6.59	9.41	
VICTORIA CLOCK TOWER	–	10.45	1.40	4.29	7.14	9.56	
HYDE PARK CORNER	–	10.51	1.46	4.35	7.19	10.01	
MARBLE ARCH	–	10.57	1.52	4.41	7.24	10.06	
BAKER STREET STN.	–	11.03	1.58	4.47	7.29	10.11	
SWISS COTTAGE	–	11.11	2.06	4.55	7.37	10.19	
CHILDS HILL	8.34	11.20	2.15	5.04	7.46	10.28	
GOLDERS GREEN	8.38	11.24	2.19	5.08	7.50	10.32	

LONDON TRANSPORT EXECUTIVE
THE ROUTEMASTER – PROGRAMME OF OPERATION
SUNDAY – COMMENCING 12 FEB. 1956.
RUNNING NUMBER W.1

CRICKLEWOOD GARAGE	7.26									
GOLDERS GREEN	–	8.56	11.31	12.53	2.15	3.38	5.01	6.29	9.08	10.32
CHILDS HILL	7.34	9.00	11.35	12.57	2.19	3.42	5.05	6.33	9.12	10.36
SWISS COTTAGE	7.43	9.09	11.44	1.06	2.28	3.52	5.15	6.43	9.22	–
BAKER STREET STN.	7.50	9.16	11.51	1.13	2.35	3.59	5.22	6.50	9.29	–
MARBLE ARCH	7.55	9.21	11.56	1.18	2.40	4.04	5.27	6.55	9.34	–
HYDE PARK CORNER	8.00	9.26	12.01	1.23	2.45	4.09	5.32	7.00	9.39	–
VICTORIA CLOCK TOWER	8.05	9.31	12.06	1.28	2.50	4.14	5.37	7.05	9.44	–
VICTORIA GARAGE	8.07	–	12.08	1.30	2.52	4.16	5.39	–	9.46	–
BRIXTON STATION	–	9.44	–	–	–	–	–	7.19	–	–
WEST NORWOOD	–	9.55	–	–	–	–	–	7.30	–	–
CRYSTAL PALACE	–	10.07	–	–	–	–	–	7.42	–	–

CRICKLEWOOD GARAGE										10.44
CRYSTAL PALACE	–	10.14	–	–	–	–	–	7.52	–	
WEST NORWOOD	–	10.25	–	–	–	–	–	8.03	–	
BRIXTON STATION	–	10.36	–	–	–	–	–	8.14	–	
VICTORIA GARAGE	8.11	–	12.11	1.34	2.56	4.19	5.43	–	9.52	
VICTORIA CLOCK TOWER	8.13	10.49	12.13	1.36	2.58	4.21	5.45	8.28	9.54	
HYDE PARK CORNER	8.18	10.54	12.18	1.41	3.03	4.26	5.50	8.33	9.59	
MARBLE ARCH	8.23	10.59	12.23	1.46	3.08	4.31	5.55	8.38	10.04	
BAKER STREET STN.	8.28	11.04	12.28	1.51	3.13	4.36	6.00	8.43	10.09	
SWISS COTTAGE	8.35	11.11	12.35	1.58	3.20	4.43	6.07	8.50	10.16	
GOLDERS GREEN	8.48	11.24	12.48	2.11	3.34	4.57	6.21	9.04	10.30	

Detail from the Central Area Bus Map (1956). The route of the number 2 bus can be traced from Finchley Road (top left of portion shown) through Park Road–Baker Street–Park Lane–Grosvenor Place–Vauxhall Bridge Road–South Lambeth Road–Stockwell Road to Railton Road (bottom right of portion shown), en route to West Norwood and Crystal Palace

REGENTS PARK
MARYLEBONE
PADDINGTON
HYDE PARK
The Serpentine
GREEN PARK
ST. JAMES'S PARK
MUSEUMS
THAMES
RIVER
PIMLICO
Pleasure Gardens
BATTERSEA PARK
BATTERSEA
STOCKWELL
CLAPHAM
CLAPHAM JUNCTION
BRIXTON
CLAPHAM COMMON

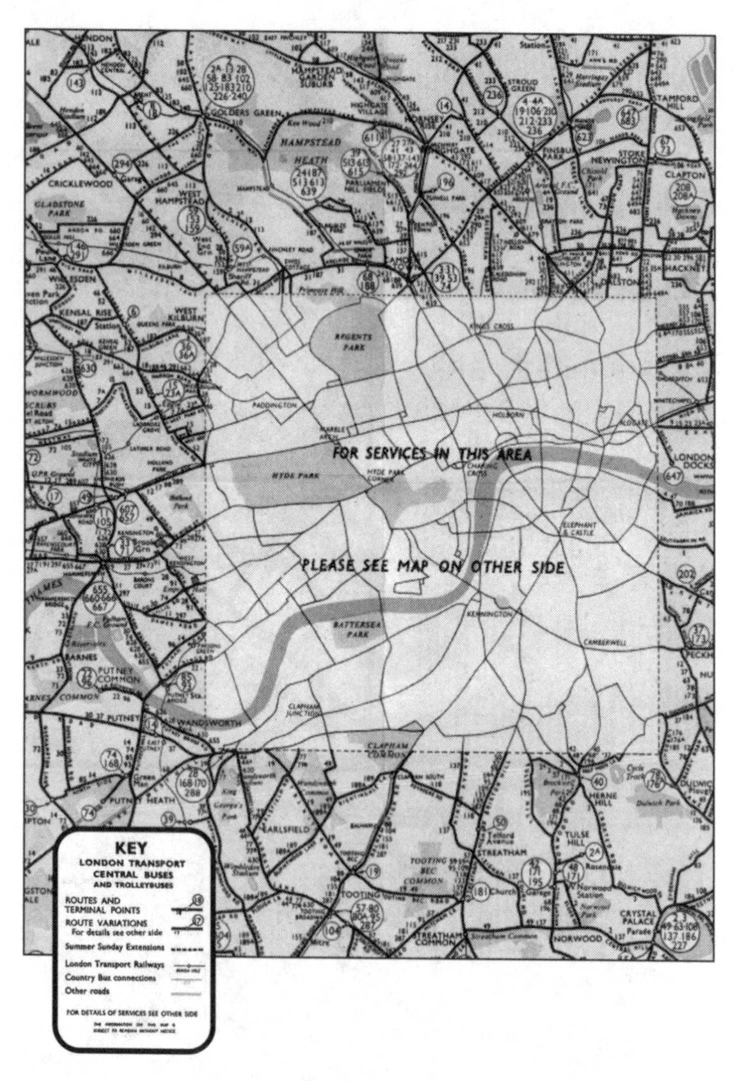

Further detail from the Central Area Bus Map (1956). Note terminal points of route number 2 at Golders Green and Crystal Palace

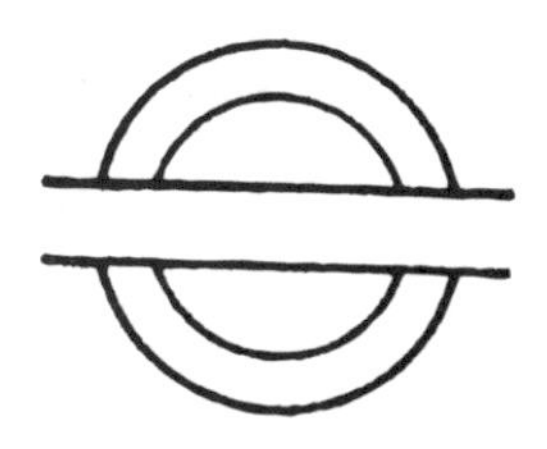

COMMENTS, SUGGESTIONS & CRITICISMS
MEMORANDUM FOR THE EXECUTIVE (1956)

SUBMITTED BY:	CHIEF PUBLIC RELATIONS OFFICER
SUBJECT:	ROUTEMASTER BUS
DATE:	25TH APRIL 1956

THIS BUS is the forerunner of the future London bus and is on trial to test its general performance and suitability.

It is of lightweight construction, embodying special features contributing to your riding comfort.

If you would like to make any comments on the 'Routemaster,' please send them to the Public Relations Officer, 55 Broadway, S.W.1.

The new Routemaster bus was put into public service on Route 2 on 8th Feb 1956. The invitation to the public to comment on the bus resulted in 61 letters being received up to 21st April and the comments are summarised overleaf:–

	Suggestions	Criticism	Appreciation
Windows			
Ventilation		12	2
Design			3
Absence of eaves to prevent rain entering		1	
Projecting window handles		1	
Seating			
Resiliency		11	3
Arrangement			7
Insufficient leg room		5	
Higher seat backs	1		
Small seat for conductor's use	1		
Substitution of crosswise seat for longitudinal	1		
Gangway width			5
Space available for conductor			1
Engine			
Noise of transmission		9	
Quietness of transmission			3
Gear changing		5	
Acceleration			2
Vibration		6	2
Design			
Appearance		2	18
Colour scheme		1	6
Design, position and size of indicator blinds		6	1
Design of heater		2	
Position of radiator		1	
Position of fareboard		3	1
Lowness of upper deck roof		1	
Suspension		5	15
Heating	2		3

Misc…			
Potential danger of position of grab rail at rear of top deck		1	
Lack of entrance door		1	
Lack of handrail near entrance platform		1	
Traffic indicators			3
Lack of bell pull on top deck		1	
Position of advertisements		1	
Suggestions			
Provision of:			
Two boxes on platform for used tickets	1		
Ash trays	1		
Loudspeaker to announce stopping places	1		
Additional luggage space	1		
Substitution of:			
Staircase with two landings, or 'B'-type stairs	3		
Lower step from platform to lower saloon	1		
Fluorescent lighting	1		
Convertible open top bus	1		
Reposition the name 'Routemaster' above L.T. sign	1		
Vehicle to be designed with seating capacity of 100	1		
Bus to be exhibited at Goodwood/Brighton Coach Rally	1		
	Suggestions	**Criticism**	**Appreciation**
Total	**18**	**76**	**75**

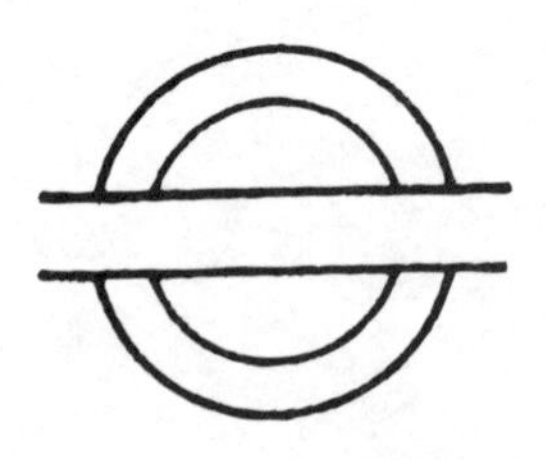

USE OF ROUTEMASTER BUSES
MEMORANDUM FOR THE EXECUTIVE (1956)

SUBMITTED BY	CHIEF MECHANICAL ENGINEER (ROAD SERVICES) OPERATING MANAGER (CENTRAL ROAD SERVICES) OPERATING MANAGER (COUNTRY BUSES & COACHES) CHIEF FINANCIAL OFFICER
SUBJECT:	USE OF ROUTEMASTER BUSES.
DATE:	21ST JUNE 1956

Introduction

It is proposed to use the newly designed Routemaster bus in substitution for existing trolleybuses. The Routemaster has many entirely new features compared with the RT buses and other contemporary vehicles and will be rather more costly to buy, but substantial economies will be obtained from its use, and it is also expected that the Routemaster bus will eventually be used when the time comes to commence the replacement of the present RT fleet. This memorandum therefore gives a technical, operating and financial appreciation of the Routemaster bus and seeks approval to the policy of using Routemaster buses to replace trolleybuses.

General Considerations.

The policy of using a specialised bus for London Transport's road services derives from a need, in the interests of economy, to maintain a high average speed of operation notwithstanding the congested state of the London streets and at the same time to incorporate in the design special features which counter the exceptional wear and tear imposed upon mechanical units by London traffic conditions, which are more severe than anywhere else in the country. Another factor in the adoption of this policy is the opportunity to which a fleet of nearly 8,000 buses and coaches, rising to nearly 9,400 when trolleybuses have been converted to oil bus operation, afford for securing the benefits by way of cheaper maintenance which flow from the precise standardisation and inter-changeability of bodies and mechanical units and all the component parts of each. Yet another consideration is the long-standing pursuit by London Transport of the "passenger appeal" of the vehicles themselves as a means of inducing travel on the public services and so countering to some extent the competition of private motoring.

A high average speed is a major factor in the economy of bus operating costs. It enables the same mileage to be run with fewer buses and therefore with fewer operating crews, fewer engineering staff to clean, service and maintain the vehicles, less garage accommodation and smaller licensing and interest and depreciation charges. At the same time a high average speed conditions the effective capacity of the streets over which the buses run. The buses must be able to keep their place in London traffic, this in London Transport's own interests as well as those of other street users.

The technical developments which permit high average speed also assist in countering the effects of traffic congestion which, in London, is not confined to one district but extends to the large number of related towns and centres which make up the London Transport Area as a whole, all of which have their local traffic problems of varying intensity. In London the buses are subjected to recurrent spells in dense traffic, often for prolonged periods, as they pass from one congested area to another, with all the stopping and starting and use of the lower gears which this involves. A powerful vehicle also assists the drivers to maintain their schedule in spite of traffic delays.

The achievement of a high average speed in London does not depend so much on high maximum speed as it does on rapid acceleration and deceleration, and these factors in turn demand powerful engines and efficient braking, with quick and easy gear changing. For these reasons the capacity of the engine in the RT bus is 9.6 litres (a capacity now frequently adopted elsewhere) instead of the more usual 7.7 litres, and air pressure braking is fitted, and to facilitate gear changing a fluid flywheel is incorporated in the transmission, together with a semi-automatic air power-actuated gear box.

The average speed of operation of the Central Buses to-day is 11.2 miles per hour, compared with 10.7 before the war, and the RT bus has undoubtedly assisted in maintaining the higher speed in spite of traffic congestion.

Another reason for a standardised bus is the fact that drivers have to change from one bus to another in the course of the same spell of duty, and it is highly desirable that all the vehicles they drive should be of similar power and performance, and that the controls and the response to them should be similar.

Furthermore, the time spent at the kerbside in loading and unloading passengers affects considerably the speed of bus operation, and, in London, where 50 per cent of the passengers carried by the Central Buses pay only the minimum fare, special attention has to be given to platforms, staircases and hand-holds to meet the traffic conditions.

The heavy wear and tear imposed on mechanical units by London traffic conditions has already been mentioned. The engine of a bus is wearing out even when it is idling and the wear and tear of both engine and transmission is accentuated when the lower gears are being used. In London, idling in traffic, gear changing and running on the lower gears are all far more frequent than elsewhere and special attention has therefore had to be given to the design of parts which are expensive to maintain and which are subject to this exceptional wear and tear. By doing so it has been possible to ensure a much longer life for mechanical units between overhaul and repair than could possibly be obtained with vehicles designed primarily for operation in provincial or country areas, and the potential physical life of the vehicles as a whole has also been lengthened, notwithstanding the onerous conditions in which they are operated.

Then, again, standardisation has led to a considerable economy in maintenance costs, both at garages and overhaul works. At the garages it has made possible a system of routine inspection and adjustment, at set intervals which correspond with the time during which each item can be allowed to run without attention, so avoiding both premature and overdue attention. The standardised vehicle has also facilitated mechanisation of servicing and cleaning.

In the workshops, with the component parts of both engineering units and bodies manufactured to strict dimensions, every part becomes completely interchangeable with another part of the same type and this has made it possible for the overhaul works at Chiswick and Aldenham to be designed on the principle of flow production common in the motor car manufacturing industry, with all the economies which flow from it. The repair of detail parts which otherwise would have to be replaced with new is also undertaken on mass-production principles.

During the years 1950 to 1955 these economies have been reflected in a reduction in the average cost of maintenance per vehicle which (at common price levels) has fallen progressively.

A further and important factor in the policy of designing a special bus for London Transport is what is called "passenger appeal". The importance of optional travel in the economics of bus operation is well-known and while a certain amount of travel outside the Monday/Friday peak hours is obligatory, a very considerable proportion of it is not. It can be short distance travel by people who "hop on a bus" instead of walking, or longer distance travel when people can be induced to make optional journeys for pleasure, entertainment or shopping purposes. The quality of the service and the vehicle have a marked effect on the extent of this optional travel.

The vehicles must be safe, reliable, comfortable, clean, well-lit, adequately and easily ventilated and capable of giving a smooth ride with the minimum of noise and fumes, if optional traffic is to be attracted and a counter be provided to the increasing competition of private motoring.

All these factors and experience with the operation and maintenance of the specialised and standardised RT bus have been taken into account in developing the Routemaster bus.

The Development of the Routemaster.

The evolution of the vehicle design now known as the Routemaster dated from early 1949 when it was deemed unnecessary to consider the type of vehicle best suited for replacing the trolleybuses at the end of their economic life.

In 1949 no decision had been taken as to whether the trolleybuses would be replaced by new trolleybuses or by oil driven buses, so that in the early stages of considering the design of the new vehicle the intention was that it should be capable of accepting either an electric traction motor or an oil engine.

Before any thought was given to the technical specification of the vehicle, a critical review was undertaken of the requirements from the traffic and operating points of view, in order to ensure that the new vehicle should approach as nearly as possible the to the conception of the ideal vehicle for the purpose required. Thus, the best basic form of the vehicle was considered, i.e. whether it should be a single-decker or a double-decker; whether there should be one or more entrances; whether an entrance should be provided at the front or the rear of the vehicle; if a double-decker, whether the staircase should be at the front or the rear, and so on.

For traffic reasons it was decided that the vehicle should be a double-decker; that the normal rear entrance and rear staircase should be retained primarily on the ground of speedy loading and unloading. Earlier experience of front entrance double-deck vehicles had been unsatisfactory because of limitations to the size of the entrance and freedom of passenger movement on entering and leaving. Furthermore, a front entrance vehicle was draughty and, in any case, would have to be provided with a door which, under conditions of city traffic and short distance riding, would seriously reduce the average running speed.

The matter of optimum passenger complement received serious and lengthy consideration and, as a result, a maximum of 65 seats with capacity for 5 standing was laid down. This limit was imposed on the two grounds of speed of loading and unloading and fare collection under peak loading conditions.

Although consideration as regards vehicle dimensions as determined by traffic considerations was reviewed without any regard to legal dimensions then obtaining, it was concluded that the vehicle should be kept as short as possible for the sake of manoeuvrability both as regards street cornering and to gain access to kerbside stopping places in the presence of adjacent vehicles including parked cars. Experience with the 500 RTW 8ft wide buses had proved this width to be helpful as regards movement in the vehicle, particularly for the conductor in collecting fares. A width greater than 8ft however, would lead to passing difficulties in congested throroughfares.

It was found practicable, without sacrifice of existing London Transport minimum seat spacing, to accommodate 64 seated passengers (28 downstairs and 36 upstairs) within the then prevailing limit of 27ft. for two-axle double-deckers, provided the engine radiator was accommodated underneath the vehicle. The first prototype built conformed to this arrangement, but as the legal length has since been increased to 30ft, it has been possible to increase the Routemaster length by 4 ins. and accommodate the radiator in the usual frontal position.

In interpreting the traffic requirements in terms of vehicle specification, the question of engine position, i.e. front, under-floor or rear was carefully reviewed. To accommodate the engine at the rear, however, would have involved loss of rear platform space, and it was desired to increase rather than reduce the platform dimensions as typified on the RT vehicle. To locate the engine beneath the floor would either have involved raising the lower saloon floor and thus increase the overall height of the vehicle which could not be tolerated owing to the limiting dimensions of railway overbridges in the London area, or, alternatively, by accepting much local obstruction in the lower saloon floor. Neither of these alternatives was considered acceptable, particularly as past experience of full-fronted double-deck operation in London had proved this to be unsatisfactory from the point of view of driver's visibility, and since for this reason no other use could be found for the space normally occupied by the engine at the front of the vehicle, the frontal position was decided upon.

To accommodate 64 seated passengers, it was necessary to provide seats for 6 additional passengers in the upper saloon. To achieve the statutory tilting angle of 28° with this additional top load without adopting the expedient of stiffening up the road springs to the detriment of riding comfort, it was necessary to incorporate an entirely new form of suspension.

This was highly desirable for another reason, namely, the unreliability and very high cost of maintaining the conventional leaf spring arrangement. Over the life of a bus, the cost of maintaining the leaf springs is about 75% of the cost of maintaining the engine which is the most costly of all units to maintain.

At the same time it was desired to improve upon the riding comfort of the leaf spring suspension and to improve stability on cornering, etc., because of the possibility that with such improved suspension, not only would the vehicle approach more closely to the comfort standard of the private car – our principal competitor – but it might enable the vehicle to be used as a double-deck coach, a role which previous experience proved to be unacceptable in the case of the RT bus on account of its unsuitable suspension characteristics.

A reduction in weight of the vehicle was aimed at in the interests of fuel consumption, tyre wear, etc., and the adoption of an improved form of suspension which would also minimise the wracking stresses on the body and reduce the transmission of high frequency vibration to the vehicle structure rendered it practicable to employ the latest type of construction, namely, the chassisless or integral form.

Light weight structures can be fabricated in thin gauge steel sections or in high duty light alloy. Whereas light alloy for various parts of the vehicle structure has been quite extensively employed in our previous designs, e.g. body panelling, various fittings, etc., steel, often in association with timber filling, has been employed for the strength members.

In considering the material to be used for the strength members of the Routemaster structure, regard was had to the desirability of designing for long vehicle life. Of the two materials available, ferrous or non-ferrous, high duty light alloy was selected because the lower specific gravity of light alloy enables thicker sections of metal to be used, and the risk of cracking and failure resulting from rust or corrosion is reduced with the thicker section material. Although light alloy is intrinsically more costly than steel, the robust section of the light alloy strength members can be counted upon to offset the additional first cost in terms of maintenance cost over the life of the bus. In the Routemaster, no wood is used for any part of the construction, and where mated parts are not bolted together, riveting is employed.

The Routemaster thus comprises a light alloy monocoque structure with coil spring independent suspension at the front and with coil springs at the rear incorporated in a special torque bar structure which enable the points of suspension to be taken to the extreme sides of the vehicle, thus adding substantially to stability.

The coil spring assemblies are such that the springs can be replaced single handed in a very short time, although the likelihood of premature fracture is very remote.

Upon the performance of the vehicle depends its ability to maintain high average speeds and thus reduce the number of vehicles required to provide a given service. Performance is determined by engine power in conjunction with the transmission – particularly the speed with which gear changes can be effected – and also upon the powers of retardation when stopping the vehicle.

The light weight construction of the Routemaster has enabled the larger vehicle with its larger complement of passengers to be constructed within the fully laden weight of the RT bus, so that it has been unnecessary to provide a larger capacity engine to achieve similar performance. On the other hand, the Routemaster gearbox is an advance on the RT box by merit of its feature of "sustained torque", which enables gear changes to be made without releasing the accelerator pedal, so that no vehicle momentum is lost during gear changing; at the same time, any possibility of jerking caused by careless driving is eliminated.

On the RT bus air braking is employed, and therefore compressed air was used for actuating the pre-selective type of gearbox. After pre-selecting the gear, the driver engages the gear by operating the air pedal. In the case of the Routemaster, however, the gearbox is actuated hydraulically from a self-contained pump and is thus independent of the braking system. By incorporating an automatic mechanism, the correct gear is automatically engaged, thus requiring no thought or physical action on the part of the driver, and no gear change pedal has to be provided. To enable the driver to change to a lower gear in the event of emergency, however, a hand-lever of standard pattern is provided beneath the steering wheel, the movement of which enable a lower gear to be engaged directly and without preselection.

In addition to relieving the driver of attention to gear change controls, automatic transmission eliminates any shortcoming in gear control arising from carelessness on the part of the driver.

Automatic transmission is gradually becoming general both in light and heavy classes of vehicles, and will undoubtedly become a standard provision within the next 5-10 years. The Routemaster automatic transmission, possessing the advantage of "sustained torque" which gives better acceleration than any other type of transmission, possesses the further advantage of high mechanical efficiency and therefore economic consumption of fuel. This is in contrast to the hydraulic torque converter used quite extensively in the U.S.A. and on the Continent which, whilst providing automatic control has a relatively poor acceleration factor and is extravagant in fuel consumption. The additional cost of the automatic unit is approximately £50 per vehicle, and its adoption in the Routemaster is strongly recommended.

A spiral bevel rear axle drive instead of the worm drive on the RT offers higher transmission efficiency and will augment the fuel saving which results from the saving in weight of the vehicle. This saving in weight alone is estimated to economise in fuel to the extent of some £20 per vehicle per annum.

On the RT vehicles, compressed air braking is used. This system, however, is prone to some disadvantages due to dust collecting in valve mechanisms, it being impracticable to provide a sufficiently efficient air intake filter, and in very cold weather, due to freezing. These disadvantages are eliminated in the hydraulic system of power braking, and this system is therefore incorporated in the Routemaster. In addition to the advantages mentioned, the hydraulic system is also lighter in weight than the air system, and thus contributes to the general saving in weight.

Over the years, steps have been taken to relieve the driver of both physical and mental strain associated with the various controls which he has to use. Thus, the old fashioned heavy clutch pedal was replaced in the RT by a light air valve pedal which is eliminated altogether in the case of the Routemaster. The large and heavy-moving gear lever has been replaced in the RT by the finger-tip control for gear changing; with automatic gear change in the Routemaster it will be completely eliminated so far as normal use is concerned. The very heavy foot pressure originally required to apply the brakes was relieved with the introduction of the servo brake, and then reduced to negligible effort by the introduction of compressed air braking or, in the case of the Routemaster, by hydraulic braking. The control which has probably received the least attention over the years is that which is in fact in use more than the others, namely, the steering wheel. Whilst improved pivot bearings and steering column gears have bettered the position to an extent, quite a lot of effort is still required. Both full power and power assisted mechanisms are now available. The full power system, however, suffers from the disability that, in the event of failure, the driver may be unable to steer the vehicle and, for this reason, for medium weight vehicles it can be ruled out. The power assisted system, however, whilst relieving the driver of considerable effort, especially when the vehicle is being manoeuvred at very low road speed, enable the driver to control his vehicle as before in the event of power failure. As in the case of automatic gear control, assisted steering will undoubtedly become general within the next five or so years; indeed, it is already being standardised on a number of private cars. Subject to satisfactory tests operating under London traffic conditions, it is strongly recommended for adoption from the outset of production, at an additional cost of £50 per vehicle.

Another important feature for which provision has been made in the Routemaster is that of saloon heating. For a number of years now the driver has been provided with heating, and there has been pressure from the public for the provision of some means of warmth inside the buses. Interior heating is now almost standard in the motor car – our principal competitor – and is being adopted by a number of provincial bus operators in both their single and double-deck vehicles to an increasing extent.

The saloon heating provided in the prototype Routemaster consists of an air intake beneath the front destination indicator with a heat exchanger connected to the engine cooling system. Air entering the intake by "ram jet" action picks up heat from the heat exchanger and is then conducted to the upper and lower saloons. Air entry is at ceiling level in the lower saloon and floor level in the upper saloon. The air flow and temperature are controllable by the conductor, but no fans are involved. There are, therefore, no running costs and maintenance costs should be negligible. The heating unit is capable of raising the internal temperature of the saloons by some 27°F. The installation has the further merit of providing additional normal ventilation during the summer months. The ventilating unit, which is capable of effecting up to 15 air changes per hour at 20 m.p.h. is incorporated in the structure of the vehicle. The additional cost of providing the heating is £50 per vehicle.

The provision of heating in new vehicles would constitute a concession to public demand but pressure for its extension to existing vehicles could legitimately be resisted on grounds that the cost of converting existing vehicles would be quite excessive. Since the heating of public service vehicles will undoubtedly be regarded as an essential factor in passenger appeal within the next few years, its adoption in the Routemaster from the outset is strongly recommended.

Summarising, the Routemaster offers enhanced passenger appeal in terms of a much more comfortable ride resulting from the improved form of the suspension; the elimination of transmission jerks, particularly with the automatic gear change; greater freedom of movement by reason of increased gangway width and better visibility by using "quarter-drop" windows instead of "half-drop" which tend to cut across the line of vision.

For the driver, the cab design which offers excellent visibility, is much improved both as regards space and as regards the design and placing of the controls, both of these features being the outcome of comprehensive physico/medical study. Mental and physical strain upon the driver can be further reduced by the simplified gear change and power assisted steering.

For the conductor, the wider gangways materially ease the task of fare collection; the provision of a recess beneath the stairs enables the conductor to stand clear of passengers entering and leaving the saloon, thus adding to his comfort and freedom of passenger movement. The reduction of high frequency road vibration will tend to lessen fatigue. Adequate accommodation for the conductor's clothing is provided.

In designing the Routemaster, special regard was had to economy in maintenance. This not only relates to ease of access and removal of assemblies in the course of routine maintenance, but also the reduction to a minimum of alterations and additions to plant and equipment, particularly at the Overhaul Works. Thus, although the Routemaster is of chassisless construction, the current practice of repairing the body separately from the mechanical units can, nevertheless, be followed. This is achieved by providing unitary construction fore and aft whereby the front suspension, engine, etc., can be speedily removed in one unit from the front of the vehicle, and the rear axle and suspension assembly can be removed in one unit from the rear of the vehicle. The body structure, and mechanical assemblies when thus separated, can be dealt with by the processes already laid down at Aldenham for overhauling the RT fleet.

Of the four Routemaster prototypes, two have undergone type and performance testing at the Motor Industry Research Association Proving Ground at Nuneaton and at the Fighting Vehicle Proving Ground at Chobham. The testing included the assessment of structural stresses and continuous running under extreme conditions of operation and loading.

A number of points requiring attention were disclosed as a result of these tests. The principal of these was the configuration of the cantilever structure carrying the front axle and engine. This, and other points which, however, were of minor character, have received appropriate design attention.

The first prototype has, to date, performed 15,000 miles in service on Route 2 from Cricklewood Garage, and has received very favourable reports from the staff. The public, invited by propaganda notices on the bus and by press notices to furnish their comments on the new design, have responded by sending in both commendations and criticisms. Nearly all points of criticism have related to known imperfections in the prototype, e.g. noisy transmission and radiator blower drive; hard seat cushions and the like. None of these imperfections are fundamental and will be remedied in later models. Further public reports will doubtless be forthcoming when further prototypes are put into service, and will be carefully studied. from the operating angle the bus has lived up to expectations.

The performance of the three further prototypes which will be placed in service later in the year will be kept under closest observation, and this will ensure that, as far as is practicable, all weak spots in the design will be disclosed and rectified before the production vehicles enter service. Comparison will also be made between the A.E.C. and the Leyland mechanical assemblies in order that any outstanding advantages of either can, if practicable, be incorporated in both.

Operating Considerations.

The operating requirements and the way they have been met on the Routemaster vehicle have been referred to in the preceding sections.

Briefly, the Routemaster will provide a vehicle which has a greater capacity than the RT bus, thus facilitating the handling of peak loads; which, with its power-assisted steering and automatic gearbox, is easier to drive and on which the conductor's task of fare collection would be eased by the greater width and improved layout.

It is to be expected that the substitution of 64-seater oil buses for trolleybuses will mean the eventual substitution of vehicles of this size for a substantial part of the present 56-seater double-deck fleet. An examination has shown that in terms of carrying capacity, the present standard of service in the peak hours could be maintained and in the off-peak hours improved, with a smaller number of the larger vehicles and with a reduction in crews.

The Routemaster with coach seating and other coach standards will, it is hoped, also be suitable for use on the Green Line coach service, and would be available to meet increased demands in the course of the next few years. If successful as a coach, the Routemaster would also bring further economic advantages to this already profitable service where it proved practicable to sue them for replacements.

The cost of the Routemaster bus.

The cost of the Routemaster, including modifications to the prototype design and an appropriate proportion of development costs is estimated at £5,827. This compared with an up-to-date estimate of the price of the RT bus of £5,380. In regard to the difference in the price of the two vehicles of £447, the following facts are pertinent :-

> The use of light alloy to save weight means a higher material cost of about £200 per vehicle, but the fuel saving from the reduced weight alone is estimated at £20 per vehicle per annum.

The extra cost of light alloy (£200) and the automatic gear change, power-assisted steering and saloon heating (£150) alone account for nearly the whole of the added cost (£370, before allowing for developments – £77).

The Routemaster seats 14 per cent more passengers than the RT., so that the respective costs per seat are :-

RT. bus	£96
Routemaster	£91

The cubic content of the Routemaster is 17 per cent greater than that of the RT bus.

The Routemaster has been designed in conformity with the specialised flow system of maintenance, and will involve the minimum of expenditure for additional or modified maintenance equipment.

By substituting coil for leaf spring suspension the Routemaster provides enhanced comfort at lower maintenance cost; it is indeed to be expected that savings in maintenance cost generally of the Routemaster as compared with the RT bus will more than cover the higher intrinsic cost of the Routemaster vehicle.

The principal advantage of the Routemaster, however, is its greater carrying capacity – 64 seats against 56, an increase of one-seventh – with a rather smaller laden weight. It is in the reduction in the number of vehicles operated in the peak hours to carry a given volume of traffic, with all the savings in crews, licensed vehicle duty, tyres, fuel, maintenance and interest and depreciation, that large savings will be found. As shown later, every bus saved will bring an economy of £4,000 a year.

The figure of cost for the Routemaster is, of course, liable to some variation due to modifications which may be found necessary during the continuing development period before production commences.

Financial effects of using the Routemaster to replace Trolleybuses.

In the estimates which were prepared three years ago of the financial effect of the conversion of the existing trolleybus fleet (excepting for a small group of vehicles working in South-West London), comparisons were made between the estimated cost of carrying out the conversion with 64-seater buses and with 64-seater trolleybuses. These calculations showed that, financially, there was little to choose between the two methods of replacing the existing trolleybus fleet but that there were major practical advantages from the use of buses, making it desirable to carry out the replacement of the trolleybuses with oil-engined vehicles rather than with electrically propelled vehicles.

These practical advantages were fully discussed in paragraphs 4 to 8 of the Executive's memorandum of 8th February 1954 which was sent by the British Transport Commission to the Minister and on which the Minister's assent to the proposals was given. They include greater mobility in congested traffic; elimination of delays from power and other breakdowns; and greater flexibility in routeing and integration of services with consequent opportunities for economies.

Although three years have passed since the original financial estimates were prepared, it is reasonable to assume that at present price levels a similar calculation would produce similar results and that the replacement of trolleybuses by 64-seater buses would still require to be determined on practical operating and engineering rather than financial grounds.

Financial advantage of the 64-seater Routemaster bus over the RT bus.

It is, however, relevant to any proposal to adopt the Routemaster bus for trolleybus replacement purposes to consider what the effect would have been on the replacement scheme had it been decided to use 56-seater buses rather than the 64-seater Routemaster buses. These calculations show that if RT buses had been used, 220 more buses would have been needed involving an extra capital cost of nearly £600,000 and the cost of the services provided in substitution for trolleybuses would have been about £1 million a year higher than it will be with the Routemaster. This is, of course, a theoretical calculation, since it was never intended to use the 56-seater bus for trolleybus replacements, but it serves to demonstrate the financial advantage which the Routemaster bus offers compared with the RT. But though savings of the order of £1 million can be assumed from the replacement of some 1,500 trolleybuses with Routemasters instead of with RT buses, it would be wrong to assume that a proportionate saving (in relation to the number of redundant buses) could be obtained from a replacement of the whole of the existing RT fleet with vehicles of greater carrying capacity. It is reasonable, however, to expect substantial savings in the number of vehicles in service when the Routemaster, with its larger seating capacity and other advantages, goes into service in place of existing RTs, but the extent of these savings can only be determined at the time of the replacement after a detailed study of the routes and services concerned and of vehicle requirements with the alternative type of buses. From the test made above in relation to the trolleybus conversion, it is fair to say that for every bus which can be saved by the substitution of 64-seater Routemasters for 56-seater RTs, a financial saving of more than £4,000 a year would accrue to the Executive. The introduction of a 64-seater bus in place of the 56-seater RT bus may well present certain staff questions. These have been left out of account in the foregoing comments.

Conclusion.

Approval is sought for the policy of using Routemaster buses equipped with heating, power-assisted steering and fully automatic gearbox to replace trolleybuses.

[Sgd.]

CHIEF MECHANICAL ENGINEER (ROAD SERVICES)

OPERATING MANAGER (CENTRAL ROAD SERVICES)

OPERATING MANAGER (COUNTRY BUSES & COACHES)

CHIEF FINANCIAL OFFICER

LONDON EXPECTS . . .
Lord Nelson, loftily surveying the London scene from his point of vantage, has seen many generations of A.E.C.'s traverse Trafalgar Square. But the latest product of the Southall factory which has built London's buses for nearly half a century would fulfil even the great Admiral's demands of perfection and service. For the first prototype A.E.C./Park Royal "Routemaster" R.M.1, seen in this photograph, has now been joined by a fleet of R.M. buses, to replace trolleybuses, equipped with fully automatic transmission and power-assisted steering. The "Routemaster" embodies every passenger transport refinement and is indeed fit to take its place as the "flagship" of London's great fleet, whose complete reliability is accepted by every Londoner.
260

"ROUTEMASTERS" IN SERVICE

'A.E.C. Gazette', November-December 1959

NEW A.E.C. PARK ROYAL "BUSES OF THE FUTURE" INVADE THE LONDON SCENE

LONDON Transport's new 64-seater A.E.C./Park Royal "Routemaster" buses made their first full-scale appearance in public service when the fourth stage of the £10 million trolleybus conversion scheme took effect on Wednesday, November 11th.

Three trolleybus routes, totalling 26.2 miles, are affected by the scheme. They are routes 567 (Barking/West India Docks–Aldgate–Smithfield) 9.42 miles; 569 (North Woolwich–Canning Town–Aldgate) 6.95 miles; and 665 (Barking–Aldgate–Bloomsbury) 9.85 miles. Because these routes use stretches of road in common with other trolleybus services, the actual mileage of road from which trolleybuses will disappear at this stage is 6.2 miles. A number of improved facilities for passengers, made possible by the greater flexibility of diesel buses will be provided.

The conversion of these routes mean the end of trolleybus operation at Bloomsbury and Barking and along most of the length of the Barking Road. One section of the road—between Canning Town and East Ham—will still be served by other trolleybus routes not due for conversion until a later stage.

Seventy-three "Routemaster" buses were needed for the changeover—the first stage for which "Routemasters" have been used. Previous stages were carried out with standard RT type buses. The "Routemasters" have 64 seats compared with the 56 seats of the RT bus, and have independent suspension, giving exceptionally smooth riding. Other features are the provision of heating on both decks, automatic transmission, and the extensive use of aluminium to save weight and fuel.

Service details

Details of the service changes are as follows:

A new daily bus route 5 replaces trolleybus routes 567 and 665. The new service runs between Barking Garage and Bloomsbury (Red Lion Square), over the trolleybus route, via Barking Broadway, East Ham, Upton Park, Plaistow, Canning Town, Poplar and Aldgate (Gardiner's Corner). The short 300-yard section of route 567 between Clerkenwell Road and Smithfield is not being replaced as only about 50 passengers a day have been using the trolleybuses over this stretch.

A new bus route 5a runs between Clerkenwell Green, Aldgate and West India Docks all day on Mondays to Fridays to replace the present peak hour only journeys operated by the 567 trolleybuses between the docks and Aldgate. It does not run at weekends.

The new No. 5 bus service is specially strengthened by adjustments to existing bus routes 15, 23 and 40 which parallel it for parts of its route so as to give a comparable service to that provided by the 567 and 665 trolleybuses.

Bus route 15 (East Ham–Ladbroke Grove) runs to and from East Ham all day and not only in the rush hours as before. On Sundays the 15 service between the West End and districts east of Aldgate have been improved. Bus route 23 (Becontree Heath–Marylebone) is increased between Barking and Aldgate all day on weekdays, and, in an attempt to overcome the effects of West End and City traffic congestion on the eastern end of the service, the route runs in two parts on Mondays to Fridays. One section operates between Barking and Marylebone and the other between Becontree and Aldgate avoiding the worst of the in-Town congestion. Through journeys run in peak hours between Becontree Heath and Marylebone as before.

On Sundays, route 9, which has taken over the 23 service along the Barking Road, has been increased between Poplar and Aldgate.

Bus route 40 (Wanstead–Herne Hill) is increased on Mondays to Fridays between Poplar and Aldgate all day and, to reduce delays caused by traffic congestion at London Bridge and in the City, it also runs in two parts so as to give more regularity in the Wanstead area. One part runs between Wanstead station and Aldgate and the other between Wanstead Flats, Camberwell and Herne Hill.

New daily bus route 48 replaces trolleybus route 569 (North

Woolwich–Aldgate) and extends through the City and Fleet Street to Waterloo on Mondays to Fridays.

During peak hours it operates between North Woolwich and Waterloo and in the off peaks between Poplar and Waterloo. It does not run after the evening rush hour. On Saturdays it only operates special journeys for dockers between Aldgate and North Woolwich during the morning and mid-day period. On Sundays it runs up to about 2 p.m. between Aldgate and Poplar with some early morning journeys to North Woolwich.

New weekday bus route 238 runs from Becontree (Chitty's Lane) to Barking and Canning Town with peak hour extensions to Silvertown and North Woolwich on Mondays to Fridays. There is no Sunday service. This route gives people living in Barking and East Ham a direct service to the Silvertown factory area.

The all-night service provided by trolleybus route 665 is replaced by a new night bus route 284 to run between Poplar and Charing Cross. The service operates over the 665 route from Poplar to Bloomsbury and then continues to Trafalgar Square via Shaftesbury Avenue and Piccadilly. One early morning journey runs to Barking.

In the Barking area, the service to the Thames View Estate has been improved by the extension of route 193 (Chadwell Heath–Barking Broadway) into the estate in place of route 23b which is now withdrawn. The 193's have a temporary terminus at Chelmer Crescent and will move to a permanent terminus at Stapleton Way when it is made ready for buses. The section of the withdrawn 23b service between Becontree and Barking is covered by the new 238 service (Becontree–North Woolwich).

Route 169 (Barkingside–Barking Broadway) is extended to provide the journeys to the Remploy Factory once operated by route 23b.

The trolleybuses displaced are operated from two depots, Poplar and West Ham. Both depots have been converted to make them suitable for diesel bus operation, but only Poplar will go over completely to diesel buses at this stage. At West Ham, buses and trolleybuses are operated side-by-side until a later stage of the conversion scheme. Poplar operates 58 "Routemaster" buses and for the time being there are 15 "Routemasters" at West Ham. (These figures include a spare vehicle at each location.) Some 270 drivers and 50 maintenance staff at the two depots have taken special conversion courses to enable them to drive and maintain diesel buses.

THE LONDON TRANSPORT STORY...

A HALF-CENTURY OF PASSENGER TRANSPORT PROGRESS

A.E.C. 1000th Routemaster, Southall, October 16, 1961.

The handing-over of the 1000th A.E.C. "Routemaster" bus by the Rt. Hon. Lord Brabazon of Tara, G.B.E., M.C., P.C., Chairman of Associated Commercial Vehicles Ltd., to Mr. A.B.B. Valentine, Chairman of the London Transport Executive, at Southall today marks an important milestone in passenger transport history.

These two undertakings, representing one of the largest passenger vehicle operators and one of the most famous manufacturers of heavy vehicles in the world, have both grown from companies closely associated over 50 years. The links which were originally forged in 1910 have strengthened over half-a-century, and now the mention of one name automatically calls to mind the other.

Together the two organisations have pioneered bus development with the result that constant research into the many factors governing the production of such highly-specialised vehicles has maintained their position in the very forefront of the industry.

The "star performer" of today's ceremony – R.M. 1000 – reflects more than half-a-century of passenger vehicle development and is a direct descendent of the immortal "B" type bus which became famous not only as London's first standardised bus, but which also represented a degree of reliability hitherto never associated with public service vehicles... [not included here] The "Routemaster" design was devised by London Transport after extensive operational research and a critical re-appraisal of the fundamental requirements of London service. The aim was for a vehicle having high powers of acceleration and braking – with special emphasis on safety – improved stability, and a high standard of passenger appeal which was necessary to meet competition from the private car. The new bus was to be economical in operation, which involved lightweight construction, and had to meet special requirements in respect of interchangeability of parts and assembly of mechanical units so as to conform to London Transport's methods of flow production for overhaul and repair. Means to ease the driver's task under the trying traffic conditions of London were also required and these included power assisted steering, fully automatic transmission, and a driver's cab designed on ergonomic principles.

The development of the design of the "Routemaster" was a masterpiece of combined operations by engineers of London Transport, A.E.C. Ltd., and Park Royal Vehicles Ltd., grouped into a working party under the chairmanship of Mr A.A.M. Durrant, C.B.E., London Transport's Chief Mechanical Engineer (Road Services).

In this way the wealth of operating and manufacturing experience painstakingly collected over 40 years, was brought to bear upon the detailed design of the "Routemaster" bus.

In the result, a design was produced which put the "Routemaster" years ahead of contemporary practice, providing not only a vehicle particularly suited for its purpose, but fit for long reliable service without fear of premature obsolescence. The vehicle is of chassisless construction and the body structure consists entirely of light alloy, giving extreme rigidity with light weight. The suspension constitutes a complete departure from the conventional, embodying independent coil suspension at the front, with coil springs at the rear widely based on a radius sub-frame which provides extreme stability and lack of roll. Fully laden on the upper deck only, stability is still retained up to a tilt angle of 32°. A sub-frame at the front carrying the suspension, engine and steering-gear, and the rear suspension sub-frame can both be removed from the body, thus enabling these parts to be separated for purposes of overhaul.

Because of the lightweight technique employed, the unladen weight has been reduced to 7 tons 7 cwts 3 qrs for the 64-seater bus and 7 tons 14 cwts for a 72-seater version. This gives unladen weight per passenger of 253 and 235 lbs respectively. The reduction in weight, the use of fluid transmission embodying the feature of sustained torque during gear changing, coupled with the use of a spiral bevel axle in place of a worm driven axle, has resulted in the fuel consumption of the 64-seater "Routemaster" being 5% less than that of the RT bus carrying only 56 seats. The sustained torque feature of the transmission also gives an 8% improvement in acceleration without any increase in fuel consumption

The A.E.C. 590 (128 b.h.p.) direct injection vertical diesel provides adequate power for the improved performance of the new vehicle, giving long life and a high degree of reliability.

A pressure hydraulic system is provide for braking, incorporating a safety provision enabling both front and rear brakes to be isolated in the event of failure of either of them, and the system is raised to working pressure in three to four seconds. It is considerably lighter in weight than air braking, avoids any freezing difficulties and reduces the risk of trouble due to foreign matter in the pressure circuit.

A novel system of heating and venting in both saloons of the "Routemaster" has been embodied and has proved highly successful. It calls for no moving parts, and in later vehicles, constant temperature is maintained thermostatically.

To date, a total of 28 million miles has been run by "Routemasters" in London service, and all of the original aims have been achieved. The buses offer an exceptional standard of comfort for passengers, ease the task of operating crews, and give substantial advantages from the technical and maintenance points of view.

The "Routemaster" design offers great potential for double-decker coach operation, as demonstrated by trials with a coach prototype. Sixty-eight "Routemaster" double-deck coaches have been ordered by London Transport for operation on their Green Line services. This in itself is high testimony of the excellence of the "Routemaster" design as a real competitor in the field of modern luxury travel.

John Moore-Brabazon, 1st Baron Brabazon of Tara (left) and Chairman of the London Transport Executive Alexander Valentine with bus driver Edwin Bonny at the handing over of the 1000th Routemaster bus to the L.T.E. at the Associated Equipment Company (A.E.C.) works in Southall, London, 16th October 1961.

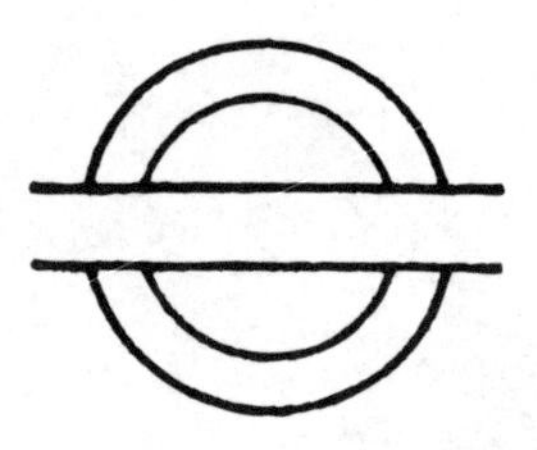

LONDON TRANSPORT'S THIRTY-FOOT ROUTEMASTER BUS LONGER 72-SEAT VEHICLES GO INTO SERVICE

London Transport Press Office, Abbey 5600 (3.11.61)

The first of London Transport's 30-ft. Routemaster buses are to go into service on November 8, from Finchley garage, on route 104 (Barnet–Moorgate). These vehicles, two-and-a-half feet longer than the normal Routemaster bus, were ordered earlier this year from A.E.C. Ltd. and Park Royal Vehicles Ltd., builders of the standard Routemaster bus.

The new buses will seat 72 passengers as compared with 64 in the present Routemasters. The order was placed so that London Transport could try out higher capacity buses under Central London conditions.

The 24 experimental 30ft. vehicles are, basically, 27-ft. 7-in. Routemaster buses modified in the later stages of construction by adding a 2-ft. 4-in. bay in the centre of the vehicle. Each of the chosen vehicles was withdrawn from the production line at a stage before the fitting of panelling and lower-deck flooring. Bolts, which had been specially used instead of the normal rivets during the assembly process to join the selected vehicles at their middle, were then withdrawn and the new bay was inserted between the separated halves of the bus.

The integral construction of the Routemaster lends itself to alterations of this kind, and the additional pillars, crossbar and hoopsticks required are all standard RM parts. All longitudinal rails, panels etc. are made from the front sections of standard No. 3 bay (third from the front) parts.

The insertion of the new bay, which has square windows on the upper or lower decks, extends the wheelbase from 16ft. 10in. to 19ft. 2in. The exhaust pipe, brake pipe and handbrake rod have been appropriately lengthened. The gearbox remains in No. 2 bay and an extension shaft supported by a bearing assembly at the new cross-member carries the drive to a modified rear cardan shaft.

The front suspension box member fitted to the 30-ft. buses is the same as that used on the A.E.C. Bridgemaster vehicles, and the front wheels have 10.00 x 20 14-ply tyres instead of the 9.00 x 20 14-ply tyres used on the standard Routemaster.

The unladen weight of the 30-ft. x 8-ft. vehicle is 7 tons 12 cwt. which gives an unladen weight per seated passenger of 235 lbs. This compares with 253 lbs. for the 27-ft. 7-in. RM, and 322 lbs. for the 26-ft. long, 8-ft. wide RTW. These buses, originally classified 'ER', are now to be known as 'RML'.

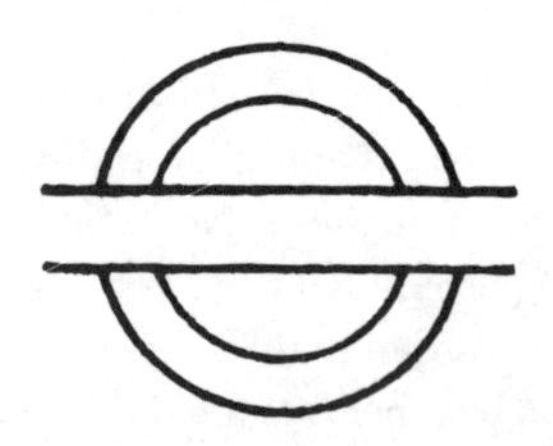

ILLUMINATED ADVERTISEMENTS ON LONDON TRANSPORT BUSES

London Transport Press Office, Abbey 5600 (29.11.63)

London Transport is to fit a number of Routemaster buses with illuminated advertisements.

Five hundred buses are to have an interior illuminated advertisement in the lower saloon. It will be on the front bulkhead just below the ceiling line and will have a visible area 29 in. long x 11 in. deep. The advertisement front is angled slightly downwards to give a better view of the display from any part of the lower saloon.

The advertisement itself is the standard type of printed paper bill and is sandwiched between two panels of clear plastic, the outer panel being framed with a moulding in a contrasting colour. This panel assembly is easily detachable, and bill changing can be effected in a matter of seconds.

The illumination is supplied by a 20W. fluorescent tube contained in a moulded plastic box assembly which combines the dual functions of a reflector unit and fascia panel. The electrical circuit is linked with the engine stop control: this ensures that the advertisement is illuminated when the engine is running and is automatically switched off when the vehicle is not in service.

As the advertisement unit will be in the position at present occupied by the saloon heater control, this control is to be moved to a new position in the vertical duct just below the advertisement. The first vehicles incorporating this modification are expected to be in service early next year.

As a further experiment, 100 of these buses will also be fitted, by next spring, with an exterior illuminated advertisement on the offside of the upper saloon where the present "banner" advertisement is displayed. This will be the same size as the present "banner", i.e. 17 ft. 6 in. long x 1 ft. 9 in. high. This advertisement is indirectly illuminated by reflected light from a continuous line of eight fluorescent tubes positioned horizontally immediately below the upper saloon waist rail in the four main bays and a vertically mounted tube in the rear bay. The total output of the fluorescent tubes is 155W.

The advertisement is in the form of a paper bill which adheres to the inner face of a continuous transparent plastic panel formed by three separate sections connected by tongued and grooved joints, the complete assembly being rubber glazed into the exterior body panels. Each section can be individually detached to allow the fluorescent tubes to be replaced. This method of presentation has the advantage of enhancing the appearance of the display during the hours of daylight, when it is not illuminated, and also protects the paper bill from dirt and from damage by washing machines.

To simplify the servicing of the electrical equipment for the exterior advertisement, the inverter units for the fluorescent tubes are grouped on a common mounting board behind the upper saloon rear nearside seat. This method has operated successfully on the Routemaster double-deck Green Line coaches which are equipped with interior fluorescent lighting. The electrical circuit has been arranged so that the advertisement is illuminated when the side and rear lights are switched on. As with the illuminated interior advertisement, the engine stop switch is used as an over-riding control to ensure that the exterior illumination is switched off when the engine is not running.

To comply with Ministry of Transport regulations, double-pole isolating switches are connected in each circuit and are located under the staircase in a readily accessible position.

The adoption of fluorescent lighting for the illuminated advertisements will not affect the saloon and indicator box lighting which will continue to be of the standard incandescent type.

RM type bus
scale 7mm = 1 foot

Length: 8395 mm (330.5 in)
Width: 1837 mm (72.36 in)
Height from road (unladen): 4381 mm (172.5 in)

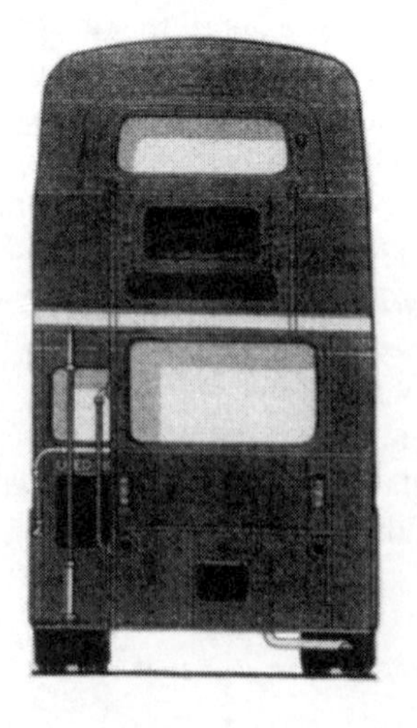

Advertising spaces
Side: 5334 mm × 546 mm (210 in × 21.5 in)
Front and rear: 508 mm × 762 mm (20 in × 30 in)
Lower rear: 1219 mm × 508 mm (48 in × 20 in)
Target: 483 mm (19 in diameter)

All lettering in white Johnston medium
Type number: 63.5 mm (2.5 in)
Legal address: 25.4 mm (1 in)
Roundel: 431.8 mm (17 in diameter)

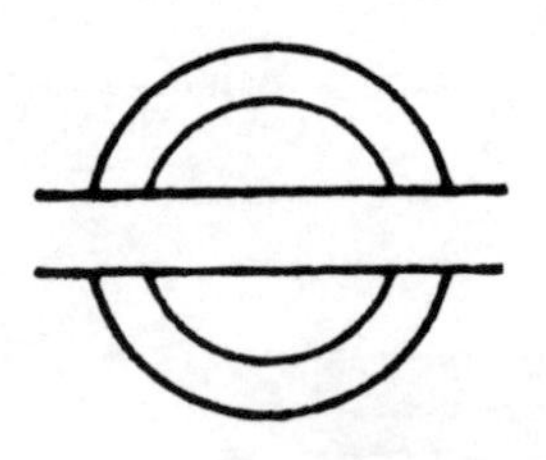

THE LONDON TRANSPORT ROUTEMASTER VEHICLES

LT Routemaster Buses: A Technical Description,
A. A. M. Durrant (1964)

INTRODUCTION

The Routemaster bus was developed by London Transport in association with the A.E.C. Ltd. (mechanical units) and Park Royal Vehicles Ltd. (body) after extensive operational research (involving four prototype vehicles) and a critical re-appraisal of the fundamental requirements of the conditions peculiar to London.

The aim was for a vehicle having high powers of acceleration and braking – with special emphasis on safety – improved stability and a high standard of passenger appeal.

The new bus was to be economical in operation, which involved lightweight construction, and had to meet special requirements in respect of interchangeability of parts, and assembly of mechanical units, so as to conform to London Transport's methods of flow production for overhaul and repair. There are four double-deck versions of the Routemaster vehicle, all of which are of a nominal 8' 0" wide.

There is a standard bus with seats for 64 passengers and a luxury coach to seat 57, both being 27' 7" long. The entrance to both vehicles is at the nearside rear, the bus has the conventional open type platform, whereas the coach has electrically operated folding doors.

The other two RM versions are 30ft. long, which, by reason of their independent front and rear mechanical units, has readily been accomplished by the introduction of an additional 2' 4" bay central between the front and rear bulkheads. On of these two vehicles, which seats 72 passengers, has the conventional open type of rear platform, but the other vehicle is a forward entrance version with electrically operated folding doors and seats 69 passengers.

Whereas the standard 27' 7" long bus and coach are in normal service, the two 30ft. variations are in experimental service to test their suitability under some of the conditions met in London.

In addition to the four versions of the Routemaster vehicle detailed in Sections 1–4 inclusive, fifty 30 ft. long "Green Line" double deck coaches have been ordered to cater for the increased commuter traffic requiring fast luxury coach service over the present East London routes now served by the 26 ft. long RT double deck vehicles.

The body is to incorporate the additional centre bay similar to the present 30 ft. long RML and RMF buses.

All the luxury features at present embodied in the existing 27' 7" long RMC type "Green Line" double deck 57 seater coach, detailed in section 2, are included in this new vehicle, but the seating capacity will be increased by 8, to a total of 65.

The increased weight of this vehicle coupled with the necessity for a higher average speed for coach services will require a power unit of greater maximum torque than the present standard 9.6 litre RM engine. As a consequence, an A.E.C. 11.3 litre engine is to be installed in this vehicle, which in overall dimensions and mounting is the same as the A.E.C. 9.6 litre version except that the cylinder liners and pistons are larger to provide the increased power required.

As a result of operating experience since the RM vehicle was first placed into service at the end of 1959, various detail modifications continue to be introduced and as such it should be noted that the information contained in this booklet is applicable only to the latest type of vehicle entering service up to January, 1964.

26th February, 1964.

COMPARATIVE TABLE: RT, RM, RMC, RML, RCL, RMA & FRM TYPES

			EX L.C.B.S.		EX L.C.B.S.	EX B.E.A.	
	RT	RM	RMC	RML	RCL	RMA	FRM
CHASSIS OR MECHANICAL UNITS	A.E.C. LTD.						
BODY MANUFACTURER	PRV / MCW	PARK ROYAL VEHICLES LTD.					
TYPE OF CONSTRUCTION	composite body on chassis	ALUMINIUM ALLOY – INTEGRAL					
LENGTH – overall	7918	8396		9107		8396	9544
WIDTH – overall	2286	2438					
HEIGHT – maximum unladen	4351	4383	4380	4393	4397	4383	4413
WHEELBASE	4978	5131		5842		5131	
OVERHANG – front	654	878				876	2159
OVERHANG – rear	2286	2388					2242
TRACK WIDTH – front	1918	2035					2057
TRACK WIDTH – rear	1761	1861					1905
GROUND CLEARANCE – laden	127	181	X	181	X	X	X
GROUND CLEARANCE – front valance (laden)	X	337				X	305
TURNING CIRCLE DIA. outer front wheel	17399	17678		19888		17526	
TURNING CIRCLE DIA. inner rear wheel	9931	9449		11049		9347	
SWEPT TURNING CIRCLE DIAMETER	18237	18364		20599		18364	20422
MAIN SALOON FLOOR HEIGHT FROM GR[nd] unladen	716	731	720	741	722	X	711
STEP HEIGHT – entrance: FIRST	389	419	402	422	400	356	397
STEP HEIGHT – entrance: SECOND	276	273	273	273	273	2 STEPSa175	273
STEP HEIGHT – exit: FIRST							
STEP HEIGHT – exit: SECOND							
ENTRANCE DOORWAY WIDTH – between handrails			1035		959	978 NO HANDRAILS	SPLIT ENTRANCE 546 BOTH SIDES
EXIT DOORWAY WIDTH – between handrails							
LOWER SALOON HEADROOM (MAXIMUM / MINIMUM)	1811	1820	1823	1820	1823	1823	
UPPER SALOON HEADROOM	1743	1743	1746	1743	1746	1743	
TILT TABLE ANGLE – WHEELS	28°	28°		29°		X	29°
TILT ANGLE – BODY	36°	33°		33°		X	33°
UNLADEN WEIGHT PER WHEEL: N/S FRONT	1581	1651	1728	1831	1797	X	1549
UNLADEN WEIGHT PER WHEEL: O/S FRONT	1635	1778	1741	1842	1930		1080
UNLADEN WEIGHT PER WHEEL: N/S REAR	2051	1937	2121	1885	2210	X	2807
UNLADEN WEIGHT PER WHEEL: O/S REAR	2219	2146	2331	2261	2318		3416
UNLADEN WEIGHT PER AXLE: FRONT	3216	3429	3477	3678	3728	3537	2629
UNLADEN WEIGHT PER AXLE: REAR	4271	4083	4452	4146	4528	4521	6223
UNLADEN WEIGHT – TOTAL	7487	7512	7928	7824	8255	8058	8852
LADEN WEIGHT PER WHEEL: N/S FRONT	2321	2445	2425	2761	2689	X	2296
LADEN WEIGHT PER WHEEL: O/S FRONT	2270	2489	2445	2711	2673		1997
LADEN WEIGHT PER WHEEL: N/S REAR	3375	3283	3369	3294	3509	X	4572
LADEN WEIGHT PER WHEEL: O/S REAR	3343	3480	3423	3765	3616		4687
LADEN WEIGHT PER AXLE: FRONT	4591	4934	4867	5472	5363	4126	4293
LADEN WEIGHT PER AXLE: REAR	6719	6712	6792	7060	7125	7615	9259
LADEN WEIGHT – TOTAL	11310	11646	11659	12532	12488	11741	13552
WEIGHT OF PASSENGERS, DRIVER AND CONDUCTOR	3683	4191	3787	4699	4255	3619 NO CONDUCTOR	4699 WITH CONDUCTOR
UNLADEN WEIGHT PER PASSENGER – kg.	134	115	136	107	124		120
SEATING CAPACITY – TOTAL	56	64	57	72	65	56	72
SEATING CAPACITY – upper saloon	30	36	32	40	36	32	41
SEATING CAPACITY – lower saloon	26	28	25	32	29	24	31
STANDING PASSENGERS ALLOWED	5	5	5	5	5		3
ENGINE TYPE	9.6L 115bhp at 1800 r.p.m.	9.6L 115bhp at 1800 r.p.m.	9.6L 150bhp at 1800 r.p.m.	11.3L 115bhp at 1800 r.p.m.	11.3L 150bhp at 1800 r.p.m.	11.3L 175bhp at 2200 r.p.m.	11.3L 150bhp at 1800 r.p.m.
TRANSMISSION SYSTEM	PRE-SELECT 4 SPEED	AUTOMATIC EPICYCLIC	SEMI-AUTO 4 SPEED	AUTOMATIC EPICYCLIC	SEMI-AUTO 4 SPEED	AUTOMATIC EPICYCLIC	
BRAKE SYSTEM	AIR PRESSURE ASSISTED	HYDRAULIC CONSTANT FLOW					
SUSPENSION ARRANGEMENT: FRONT AXLE	LEAF SPRING	COIL SPRING	COIL SPRING	COIL SPRING	COIL SPRING		
SUSPENSION ARRANGEMENT: REAR AXLE			AIR SPRING		AIR SPRING		
TYRE SIZE & MINIMUM PLY RATING: FRONT	9.00-20 12 PLY	9.00-20 14 PLY		9.00-20 14 PLY		9.00-20 12 PLY	9.00-20 10 PLY
TYRE SIZE & MINIMUM PLY RATING: REAR	9.00-20 10 PLY	9.00-20 10 PLY		9.00-20 10 PLY			9.00-20 14 PLY
FUEL TANK CAPACITY – GALLONS	35	29	41	29	42	X	46
WATER CAPACITY – GALLONS	7	8	8	8	8	8	11
STEERING	WORM & NUT	WORM & NUT – POWER ASSISTED					
DOORWAY CONFIGURATION	OPEN REAR PLATFORM		REAR PLATFORM JACK-KNIFE DOORS	OPEN REAR PLATFORM	OPEN REAR PLATFORM	REAR PLATFORM JACK-KNIFE DOORS	COMBINED FRONT ENTRANCE/EXIT
DOOR CONTROL			ELECTRIC			ELECTRIC	

WEIGHTS ARE GIVEN IN KILOGRAMS

NOTE: CERTAIN L.T. VEHICLE TYPES ARE MANUFACTURED TO METRIC DIMENSIONS. FOR EASE OF COMPARISON ALL TYPES ARE DETAILED IN THE EQUIVALENT METRIC DIMENSIONS ON THIS CHART.

1. THE STANDARD ROUTEMASTER DOUBLE DECK BUS

The standard Routemaster bus which carries the code letters 'RM' is a two-axled vehicle of all-metal monocoque construction, capable of carrying 64 seated passengers, 28 in the lower saloon and 36 in the upper.

The boarding and alighting of passengers is from the nearside platform behind the rear bulkhead with a staircase to the upper saloon so designed to be of easy ascent and descent.

The driver's cab is in the orthodox position on the offside of the vehicle forward of a full fronted saloon bulkhead. Power assisted steering and a driver optional manual or fully automatic transmission is provided together with heating, ventilating and screen demister. The hand brake is placed on the left of the driving position to facilitate entry.

The bus has nominal dimensions of 27' 7" long, 8' 0" wide, with an unladen height of 14' 4⁹⁄₁₆" and a wheel base of 16' 10".

The unladen dry weight of the vehicle is approximately 7 ¼ tons, which with the weight of the 64 passengers and the driver and conductor to the current Ministry of Transport Regulations, results in a laden weight including fuel and water of a little over 11½ tons. this was accomplished by the extensive use of light alloys in the body construction, glass fibre components and other light weight materials which resulted in a passenger/weight ratio substantially lower than that of previous L.T. road service vehicles.

A combined heating and ventilation system has been provided in both the upper and lower saloons.

No conventional chassis frame is employed, the body structure serving as the main load-carrying unit with sub-frames to mount the mechanical units at front and rear, these being so arranged as to be easily removable for overhaul.

Independent coil spring front suspension and a patented form of coil spring rear suspension are used to give an effectively wider spring base which promotes vehicle stability coupled with much improved riding characteristics.

The engine, which is housed at the front of the bus to the left of the driver, has a special design of mounting to reduce the transmission of engine vibration to the body structure.

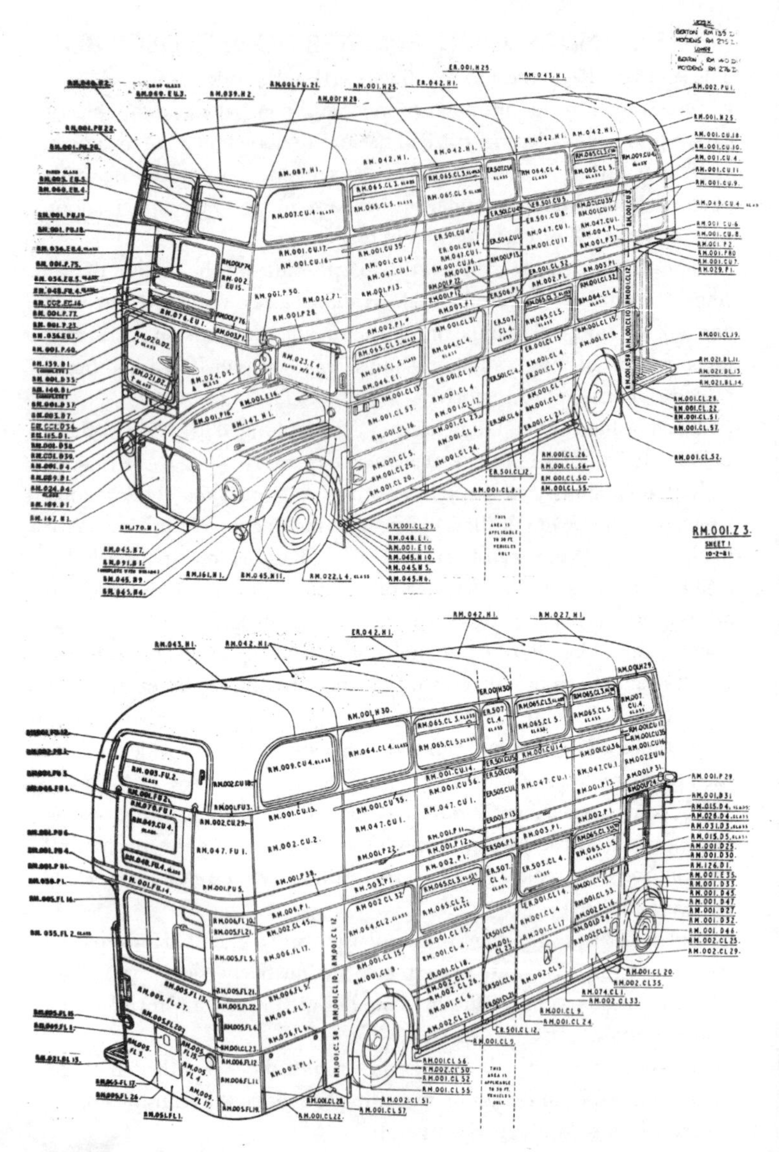

RML mechanical engineering drawings, annotated with panel and body part codes

2. GREEN LINE ROUTEMASTER DOUBLE DECK COACH – RMC

Based directly on the Routemaster bus, the new Green Line coach incorporates all the main features of the bus construction. Additions and modifications have been made, however, to suit the requirements of Green Line coach operation. The principal new features are the provision of power-operated folding doors for the rear platform, the installation of fluorescent lighting in both saloons, a higher quality of seating which has been re-spaced to give greater knee-room than in the bus and the fitting of parcels racks and provision of more luggage space. Air suspension is incorporated at the rear, direct selection of gears is provided, a higher ratio differential is fitted, and the 4-headlamp system has been adopted.

This successful adaptation of the Routemaster has brought considerable advantages both in regard to manufacture, where comparatively little special tooling has been necessary, and in maintenance and overhaul procedures, and it carries London Transport's policy of vehicle standardisation one stage further. The integral-construction bodies, nominally 27' 7" long x 8' wide, were built by Park Royal Vehicles Ltd., and the sub-frames, engine and running units by A.E.C. Ltd.

The doors fitted to the rear platform are double jack-knife, electrically-operated units. The side destination box above the rear platform has been raised to accommodate the door-operating gear, access to which is obtained through an external hinged flap. The doors are normally opened by the driver. Operating buttons are located on the nearside wall of the driver's cab, and a warning light is illuminated when the doors are in the open position. A conductor's control for closing the doors is situated on the nearside of the rear bulkhead, and emergency control buttons for opening the doors from the interior or exterior are also provided. Also for emergency use, a pull handle is provided on the inside of the doors, and from the outside they can be pushed open manually.

An emergency door for the lower deck is situated at the rear of the vehicle at the foot of the stairs.

The enclosure of the rear platform has made necessary minor

alterations to hand rails, and the position of the used ticket and registration number boxes, as well as the re-positioning of the side destination box, access to the winding handle of which is now obtained from the upper saloon.

Although the incandescent lighting used on the Routemaster bus is considered adequate for short-stage operation, a higher level of illumination is desirable for the longer distance traveller who may wish to read during the journey, and the level has been improved some 2 ½ times by the use of fluorescent lighting on the coach, without increase of load on the electrical generating and storage system.

The lower saloon has six 2-ft. 20-W. tubes, three each side at cant rail level, and in the upper saloon there are eight 2-ft. 20-W. tubes, four nearside, three offside, and one in the rear of the roof above the emergency door. These 14 tubes are driven by seven transistorised inverters (each driving two tubes in series) which are grouped together on a panel located behind the nearside rear passenger seat in the upper saloon. Destination indicators are illuminated by incandescent lighting as used on the Routemaster bus.

Seating in the coach follows the general pattern used in the bus. There are 57 seats, 25 in the lower saloon and 32 in the upper. Reduction in the seating capacity has allowed re-spacing, to give 1 ¼ in. more knee-room in the lower saloon, and 1 ¾ in. in the upper saloon. The longitudinal seats in the lower saloon have been reduced in length, and the nearside seat carries three passengers. On the offside, the conductor's locker is situated inside the saloon against the rear bulkhead, leaving space for two passengers, but re-positioning of the locker gives more luggage space under the stairs. The upper saloon of the coach has two fewer double transverse seats than the bus. The foamed-rubber/foamed-plastic laminated seat cushions and squabs are deeper than those used on the bus and are covered in a dove grey and maroon moquette. In the upper saloon ash-trays are fitted to the back of the squabs.

The interior colour scheme below the cant rail is similar to that of the bus's brown floor, maroon from floor to waist rail – but from the waist to cant rail the colour is Sung yellow, and the ceiling is white. The exterior livery follows the Green Line pattern of Lincoln green with pale green band between upper and lower decks and pale green window surrounds. On each side of the vehicle a London Transport bull's-eye plaque is disposed centrally on the upper saloon side C-frame and a bull's-eye transfer is situated at the rear above the registration number box.

The indicator display on the front differs from that of the bus in that there is no separate route number box. The box carrying the intermediate route points in repositioned symmetrically above the ultimate destination box and the blind also carries the route number. the route number box under the front nearside canopy has been omitted. The layout of the rear destination boxes is unchanged.

Parcel racks, positioned at cant rail level in both saloons, are of stainless steel tubing with detachable aluminium frames and red nylon netting. A button for the conductor's signal bell is provided on the lower platform only, both saloons being fitted with buzzers. Stanchions have been omitted, as is the practice with Green Line coaches, and the slatting in the gangways has been replaced with cork/rubber composition non-slip floor tiles. The major change in the running units is the use of air suspension at the rear in place of the standard coil springs of the Routemaster bus. Coil springs provide a better ride than leaf springs, but whereas the difference between coil spring and air suspension is not so marked as to justify the use of air for short-stage work, its use is considered justified for long-distance coach operation. The riding characteristics of the air springs are unaffected by variation in the passenger load, and the platform height is maintained at a constant level above the ground. The softer suspension also results in reduced loads from road shocks and may be expected to prolong the body life.

Rolling diaphragm suspension units were chosen after extensive testing of various types of units on prototype Routemaster bus RM1, the prototype Routemaster coach, and 50 Routemaster buses.

The air bellows are fitted in place of the rear coil springs, each being connected at its upper end to a surge tank, the additional volume of which (540 cu.in. each side) is required to give the desired suspension characteristics. Frequency is 70 cycles per min. Air pressure is supplied from the standard gearbox operating system as fitted to the bus, and is controlled by levelling valves, one each side, mounted on the underside of the body and connected to the suspension sub-frame. These valves are sensitive to relative movement between body and axle which causes inflation or deflation of the bellows as the passenger load varies. A delay period of 9 secs. makes the valves insensitive to normal road shocks and body sway when cornering. If, after standing overnight or for longer periods the pressure in the air system is low, it can be topped-up from garage mains at a point located for convenience under the bonnet. The shock absorbers, which on the bus are mounted co-axially with the coil springs, have been sited inboard of the suspension units on the coach. Half the coaches have been equipped with arm-type shock absorbers and the remainder with telescopic units similar to those on the bus.

Operating on Green Line service, the number of gear changes per mile are some 70 per cent less than on Central Area buses. Fully automatic transmission is therefore not justified and the coaches have been equipped with direct selection transmission. This uses the basic epicyclic gearbox and fluid flywheel as used on the Routemaster bus, but the solenoid-operated pneumatic valves for each gear are selected by manual operation of the change speed lever mounted on the steering column. Although provision has been made on the vehicle to automatically idle in neutral when the vehicle road speed drops below 4 m.p.h., this feature is not at present being used pending further development of the gearbox. The coach retains the spiral bevel and pinion differential as on the bus, but the ratio is 4.7:1 – similar to that now used on RF Green Line coaches.

An additional fuel tank, supplementing the standard 29-gallon tank to give a total of 41 gallons to cater for the longer mileages operated in coach service, is positioned in the bay to the rear of the standard tank.

A noticeable feature is the adoption of four headlamps which fit conveniently into the basic Routemaster frontal design.

3. 30 FT. LONG ROUTEMASTER DOUBLE DECK BUS – RML

Following on from the design of the London Transport standard Routemaster bus, which, within an overall body length of 27' 7" seats 28 passengers in the lower saloon and 36 in the upper saloon, for a total of 64, L.T. are operating in service an experimental batch of 30ft. long

RM type vehicles. These buses – code letters 'RML' – seat 32 passengers in the lower saloon and 40 in the upper saloon for a total of 72. These buses are based directly on the standard 27' 7" long bus with the aluminium alloy body of integral construction.

The mechanical and electrical running units are standard Routemaster equipment but due to their increased overall body length, a modified rear cardan shaft is required together with an additional short intermediate cardan shaft and centre bearing assembly and also a lengthened brake rod, brake pipe lines and exhaust pipe.

The increase in the body length to 30ft. was accomplished by the introduction of an additional 2' 4" bay with fixed windows central between the front and rear bulkheads.

4. 30 FT. LONG FORWARD ENTRANCE ROUTEMASTER DOUBLE DECK BUS – RMF

A further development of the 30ft. long version of the Routemaster bus RML (a brief description of which is given under section 3), is the forward entrance double deck bus which is in operation to test its suitability for service under some of the conditions met in London.

This experimental bus, code letters 'RMF', seats 31 passengers in the lower saloon and 38 in the upper saloon for a total of 69, and is fitted with electrically operated folding doors under the control of the driver.

This vehicle, like the existing 30ft. RML type, is based directly on the standard RM bus with the aluminium body of integral construction.

The mechanical and electrical running units are standard RM equipment but due to its increased overall body length, there is a modified rear cardan shaft, an additional short intermediate cardan shaft and centre bearing assembly and also lengthened brake rod, brake pipe lines and exhaust pipe. New rear suspension coil springs of increased capacity were required because of the altered weight distribution compared with the standard vehicle. The reduced weight on the front suspension allowed 9.00 x 20 tyres to be used instead of 10.00 x 20 tyres on the existing 30ft. RML buses.

The increase in the body length to 30ft. was accomplished by the introduction of an additional 2' 4" bay in the centre of the vehicle similar to that adopted on the RML bus.

The positioning of the passenger entrance and staircase in the front bay of the lower saloon entailed structural alterations to both ends of the standard body. The first and second bays of the side frame of the upper saloon over the new entrance are strengthened to compensate for the loss in the lower saloon frame; at the rear, in the spring mounting area, the lower half of the rear bulkhead structure is retained and strengthened to carry the extra weight on the rear end. The sections of the body structures affected are therefore built as far as possible in the normal way, using existing jigs and parts, and then completed with the modifications before being assembled with the rest of the body structure.

At the rear, the nearside side frame and rear frame have been extended to enclose the rear corner, and additional lower saloon windows have been introduced. The lower saloon floor has been extended; at the height of the longitudinal seat footstools, across the rear bay. The extra height of the floor in this rear bay allows a completely enclosed underfloor battery compartment to be provided beneath it and the rear seat. Access to the compartment is given by a detachable external panel.

An emergency exit in the offside of the lower saloon is situated just forward of the rear seat. When this exit door is opened a warning bell rings in the driver's cab.

The normal nearside route blind box is omitted from the RMF and the standard rear blind gear assembly is modified to allow the blind to be adjusted through a trap in the ceiling of the lower saloon: the blinds can be changed by removing the centre cushion of the rear five-passenger seat in the upper saloon.

The two-step passenger entrance is fitted with double jack-knife doors, electrically operated. These doors are normally opened by the driver and closed by either the driver or the conductor. There are internal and external control buttons for emergency use; for emergency manual operation, there is a pull handle on the inside of each door. The door mechanism is in the upper saloon under the nearside seats above the doors and is completely enclosed, access being through a detachable plate. There is a seven-step semi-spiral staircase to the rear of the front bulkhead with the lower steps facing the entrance. The rear of the staircase is enclosed by a partition from floor to lower deck ceiling to form the luggage compartment and conductor's locker space. Access is from the centre gangway. The conductor's locker, with door carrying the standard faretable, occupies the upper part of the under-stair space but there is a further compartment, reached through the locker, for the conductor's coat. This compartment extends downwards into the luggage space, from which it is separated by a hinged door. The door can be opened if required to give more luggage space. On the locker door, below the faretable, is a horizontal foam-rubber-filled back rest for the conductor, and the saloon lighting switches are beneath the locker.

The offside route number box in the first bay of the side frame structure was fitted originally but was subsequently removed in the interest of safety. A double-skinned nearside partition, glazed above the waist, accommodates the conductor's bell push, waybill holder and, above the window, the door closing and emergency opening buttons. A box for used tickets is fitted to the front of this partition, and the mouth of this box has been arranged to form a grab rail. There is a second used ticket box on the nearside of the front bulkhead. The front bulkhead, below waist level, is a standard Routemaster structure but above the waist it is modified to embody a special fixed window on the nearside and a stress panel on the offside. The fixed window is in two sections. The inner section is set at a forward angle to meet a repositioned cab pillar so that a clear view of the entrance doors is provided for the driver to the rear of the pillar. A special curved Perspex window is fitted between this pillar and the bulkhead and the repositioned cab pillar necessitates the use of a reduced length driver's emergency window. A folding type leathercloth blind with peep hole is provided inside the cab to screen the curved window for night driving. The bonnet has been shortened to clear the angled window and an aluminium cowling is fitted to fill the gap. This cowling is detachable to facilitate removal of the nearside window structure.

The standard Routemaster heating and ventilating system is employed but with a modified pipe run to suit the repositioned nearside cab pillar. The air ducting is modified with the lower saloon outlet located under the front bulkhead header panel. The standard saloon heater control unit, but with a flat encutcheon, is mounted in the normal position on the interior bulkhead header panel.

Two extractor ventilators are installed in each saloon. These are in the rearmost nearside and offside lower saloon bays above the windows and directly above the upper saloon rear emergency window.

In general, the standard transverse bus seat arrangement and spacing is used but the lower saloon longitudinal seats are extended to the rear of the wheel arches to accommodate five passengers each. In addition, five-passenger transverse seats are introduced at the rear of both lower and upper saloons and three single seats are sued in the upper saloon, the two facing forward on the nearside opposite the staircase being fitted with guard rails. The third, facing the centre gangway at the rear of the staircase fender panel, is fitted with a "pickpocket panel". The existing bus type of seat frame, squab filling and trimming, are used throughout, with stainless steel handrails and stanchions. 'Doverite' covering is fitted to the two exterior vertical handrails and the vertical portion of the interior handrail attached to the bulkhead.

Fixed and quarter-drop window assemblies are used, as on other Routemaster vehicles, but with the lower saloon drop windows repositioned to suit the revised entrance and staircase layout. There are additional small fixed windows in both saloons in the centre bay, as on the 30ft. long RML vehicles, and two more in the lower saloon offside rear bay, one of which is in the emergency door. The transverse rear lower saloon is wider than in other Routemasters.

Standard Routemaster bus lighting is embodied with the addition of lamp positions over the rear upper and lower saloon transverse seats and twin lights over the entrance stepwell. The nearside upper and lower saloon lighting circuits are interconnected by relays to the engine stop control switch so that these lamps are extinguished, in order to conserve the batteries when the vehicle is stationary with engine stopped.

The interior finish conforms to the bus standard in that the saloon floors and staircase are "Treadmaster" covered, but multi-slats replace individually fixed slats. The colour scheme is principally dark burgundy from floor to waist, with Chinese green from waist to cant rail and Sung yellow ceilings.

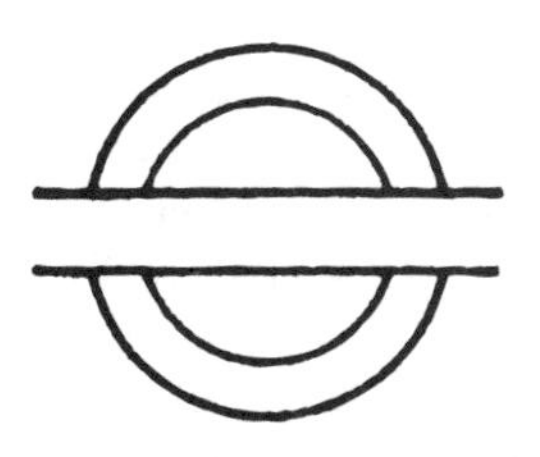

ROUTEMASTER BUSES

INSTRUCTIONS FOR DRIVERS AND CONDUCTORS

Revised Edition, May 1964

The Routemaster is basically different in design from the RT bus. It is of chassisless construction manufactured in light alloy with coil spring independent suspension at the front, and a coil spring suspension at the rear specially designed to ensure stability. The vehicle incorporates fully automatic transmission with over-riding control; power assisted steering; high efficiency power hydraulic braking; with fresh air heating and ventilation on both decks.

FOR THE DRIVER

STARTING THE ENGINE

First check that the handbrake is hard "on", that the gear selector lever is in neutral, and that the engine stop control is pushed fully home. Press the accelerator pedal right down and operate the starter switch until the engine fires. Release switch as soon as engine fires, release pedal and engine will idle.

DRIVING THE VEHICLE

The transmission changes gear automatically according to conditions of road speed and accelerator pedal position.

To move off, place the gear selector lever in the normal top gear position. Release hand-brake against the pull-away of the vehicle. The vehicle may then be driven solely by use of the accelerator and brake pedals.

It is particularly important that the handbrake should be applied each time the vehicle is stopped to prevent it running backward or forward. Such movement is likely on a slight slope.

When descending hills which are scheduled for descent in low gear, or in any other abnormal circumstances, the required gear should be engaged manually. While the selector gate is similar to that on the RT bus, third and top gears cannot be engaged unless the vehicle is in motion; first and second gears can be engaged manually when the vehicle is stationary and at relevant road speeds. Reverse gear must only be engaged when the engine as at idling speed and the vehicle is stationary with the handbrake on. When manoeuvring in garages or confined spaces, drivers should use the second speed manual gear, and not the automatic.

In the event of the rear wheels skidding, a relay trips in the automatic mechanism causing neutral to be engaged. The drive can be restored by stopping the vehicle and depressing the selector lever down through the gate with the reverse catch pulled and held there for 10 seconds. In no circumstances must the accelerator be pressed while so doing. If this action is not successful, then the garage must be telephoned for instructions. For emergency operation, first, second and third gears will still be obtainable manually. The power assisted steering must not be turned while the vehicle is stationary.

The power hydraulic braking is very responsive to pedal movement and is lighter in application than the RT air brake. It is best operated by keeping the heel in contact with the floor plate.

PRESSURE INDICATORS

Low brake pressure is indicated, as in the case of the RT bus, by means of a white light and a warning flag. A separate indicator in the form of a red light gives warning of low gearbox pressure. When either warning is given the vehicle should be stopped and the engine revved up in neutral for 30 seconds. If either the brake or gearbox indicators fail to respond, then contact should be made with the garage.

WHEN LEAVING THE VEHICLE

Apply the handbrake, select neutral gear on the gear change lever and pull the engine stop control, leaving it in the "out" position.

FILLING THE RADIATOR

Standard Rubber Stamp

The water level in the radiator should be checked by means of a separate push button level cock, which can be reached after first lifting the bonnet. If no water comes out when the button is depressed, the main filler cap should be opened with caution and the radiator topped up to the level of the filler hole. It is dangerous to stand directly in front of the filler cap. After use it is essential that the filler cap is screwed down hard.

Metal type pressure cap

Where a metal type pressure cap is fitted no attempt should be made to remove it to check the water level. With this sealed system there should be no loss of water under normal operating conditions, but, if due to a defect there is an obvious water shortage, the garage should be contacted.

EMERGENCY FUEL SHUT OFF

To turn off fuel supply in an emergency, lift bonnet and turn hand wheel in fuel line clockwise. See sketch overleaf.

SALOON HEATING

A blind is provided in the front of the saloon heater and this blind can be drawn to prevent air passing over the radiator. The blind is drawn to cover the radiator by pulling a cord with a white knob located in the corner of the driver's cab roof and locking the knob into the retaining slot in the adjacent bracket.

CAB HEATING

The cab heater is operated by moving a white painted handle which simultaneously switches on the fan and opens the vent to admit fresh air to the heater.

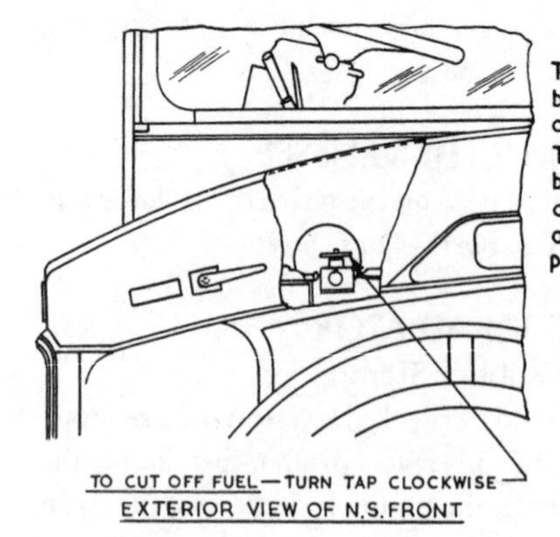

The tap will be found under the bonnet adjacent to the fuel filter on the nearside.
To cut off the fuel lift the bonnet and turn the handwheel clockwise in direction of the arrows marked on the instruction plate.

FOR THE CONDUCTOR

VENTILATION OF INTERIOR

Control is effected by moving the knob mounted on the lower saloon bulkhead. Where the knob moves horizontally, pushing it to the right increases the temperature of the air, and, in the opposite direction, decreases the temperature. Where the knob moves vertically, the air temperature is increased when the knob is moved downwards.

In the event of cold air continuing to enter the saloon after the blind has been released by the driver, with consequent discomfort to passengers, the driver should be instructed to draw the blind again which should then be left drawn throughout service. The defective system should be reported on the "Defect Report Sheet" when the bus returns to the garage.

Full fresh air ventilation is provided by the heater, when in operation, which enables windows to be closed without causing stuffiness, but windows may be opened for extra ventilation in the summer.

STAFF LOCKER

A full length coat locker for use of the Operating Staff is provided under the staircase.

THE GIBSON SELF-PRINTING TICKET ISSUING MACHINE

A User's Guide

UP TO 380 TICKETS FROM ONE ROLL

380 tickets of a size 3 ⅛" x 1 ½" can be printed. If longer tickets are required the number of tickets printed will naturally be less. The impregnated felt roller will give up to 75,000 tickets from one inking, in a temperate climate. More frequent re-inkings may be necessary in certain climates, and a re-inking aperture can be fitted when necessary (see page 127).

FAST OPERATION

A ticket is printed and simultaneously issued at high speed in the following way:

- SET THE FARE by manipulating the large wheel with the left hand. The wheel, which is large and easily grasped, is pulled outwards away from the machine. It can then be turned either way.
- SET THE CLASS with the outer small wheel with the right hand. Turn either way.
- PRINT THE TICKET by depressing the handle knob on the operating handle with the right hand, and turning it rapidly through one complete revolution.
- TEAR OFF THE TICKET upwards with the right hand, against the serrated teeth. Two tickets may be issued as one combination

ticket by tearing only after effecting the second printing. The conductor at leisure may alter the 'stage number' or the 'time' if fitted, as the bus proceeds, by moving the appropriate counter with the right hand. After each single rev. of the operating handle, the knob must be depressed before a further revolution can be started. This feature is designed to provide one hand operation of a type which automatically arranges the stop position of the operating handle, and prevents damage to the machine by careless or rough treatment.

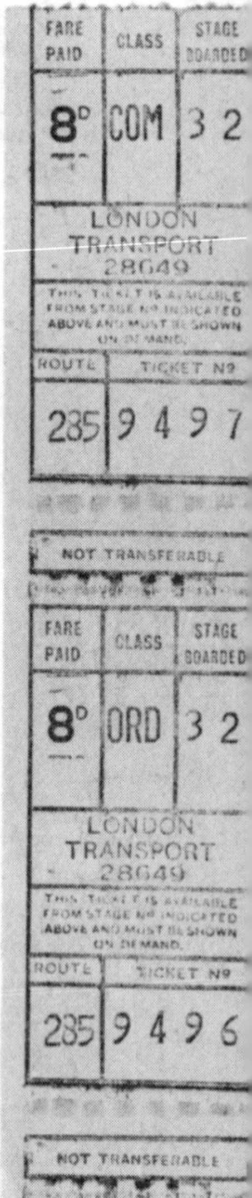

IT PRINTS AS IT ISSUES – MANIPULATED BY FINGER WHEELS (1, 2 & 3)

1. FARES

The fare selection wheel selects any one of 14 fare values, for printing on each ticket : 2d., 3d., 4d., 5d., 6d., 7d., 8d., 9d., 10d., 11d., 1/-, 2/-, 3/-, 4/-, OR .10, .20, .30, .40, .50, .60, .70, .80, .90, 1.0, 2.0, 3.0, 4.0, 5.0. For fares outside these ranges, a combination ticket must be issued (e.g., 3/- Com + 9d. Com = 3/9, OR 5.0 Com + .70 Com = 5.70). The machine can be modified to print in any currency, whether metric or not.

2. CLASS

6 classes (e.g., ORDinary, CHIld, etc.) is the standard, but the machine can be modified to be set in 12 positions which can print any 12 codes or figures (e.g., 1-12 fare stages, where the stage printer is used for another purpose).

3. FARE STAGE

The standard machine prints 1-99. It can be modified to print 1-999 or the time (1-24 hours plus the half-hours and quarter-hours).

4. ROUTE NUMBER

The standard machine prints 1-999, but can be modified to print 1-9999. It can be used to print details other than Route Number.

5. DATE

The standard machine prints day and month. It can be modified to print other alterable information or the machine number.

PRINTED AUTOMATICALLY (6 & 7)

6. TICKET NUMBER

Here the serial number of the ticket is printed. Every ticket will automatically show the total issued from that machine. The printing wheel cannot be altered and is set, on assembly, to agree with the "total tickets sold" counter (see 'Accurate Accounting').

7. MACHINE NUMBER

This fixed plate can show the machine number, some suitable device, or be left blank.

ACCURATE ACCOUNTING

1. In this window is seen the fare value (4d.), which has been set by manipulation of the large wheel by the left hand, and which will be printed. Under this large figure is seen the total of all tickets sold at that value (542).

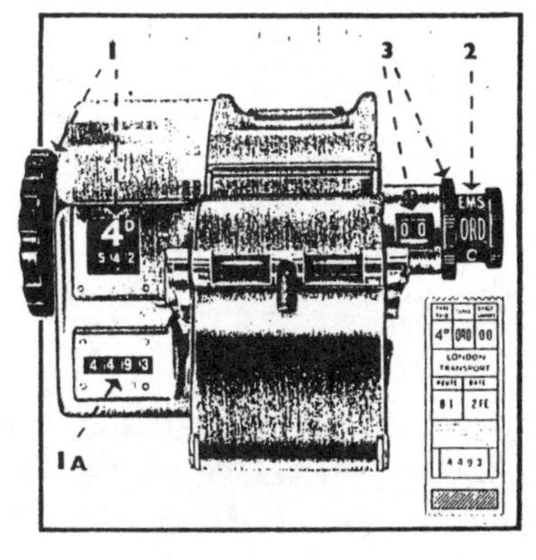

1A. In this window is seen the total of all tickets sold and the machine is set, on assembly, so that that will be identical with the serial number printed on the ticket. The sum of the increases of all 14 "totals of each fare" (1), during any period, will equal the "total tickets sold" increase, during the same period. A further feature of the machine is the use of rotary counters with a stationary striker. This gives accurate counting of fare values; the counters cannot be reversed by irregular manipulation and the drive to the counters is geared down at a 2 to1 ratio, so that counters will not jump more than the number of tickets issued, even though the conductor's operation may be unusually rapid or jerky.

2. "CLASS" selection wheel.
3. "FARE STAGE" selection wheel and aperture.

1A NOTE. The machine is self-checking, provided that the 14 fare value registers are noted at the beginning and termination of each duty. If a false reading is obtained in any of the individual fare values (1), the sum of these will not agree with the "total tickets sold" figure (1a). If the latter is altered, it will not agree ith the serial number of the ticket.

RIGID CONSTRUCTION OF POSITIVE DESIGN

This compact machine is only 7 in. high, 4 ½ in. deep and 6 in. wide, weighing 4 lb. Light alloy has been used extensively in construction for strength and resistance to wear. The casing is of 16-gauge sheet, while bearing surfaces between the value counters are also of this alloy. Elsewhere all wearing parts are of hardened and tempered cast steel. The printing drum revolves on generous bearings between two plates, and the assembly has been specifically designed to ensure concentricity of the drum in operation so that tickets are printed evenly and without distortion of details. After the initial heavy inking density has worn off, an even printing is maintained throughout the remainder of the run. The counting drum revolves easily on large capacity bearings. Thanks to the positive design and rigid form of construction, it is impossible, inadvertently or otherwise, to alter the value of a fare while the ticket is being issued.

INSERTING A NEW ROLL

A new paper roll can be fitted in less than ten seconds by the operator (while wearing the machine) in the following way:

Lift the centre catch on the lid of the spool container.

*   *   *

Lift the lid as shown in the picture.

*   *   *

Pull out the old roll.

*   *   *

Replace a new roll by pushing it in until it is gripped by springs, leaving the end of the paper out, as shown in the picture.

*   *   *

Shut the lid and depress the catch.

HARNESS & CASE

A harness is used when the machine is worn by the operator. It consists of bands of 2 in. webbing made in the form of a cross, and worn with the joint of the cross between and below the shoulder blades. All four ends are adjustable for length; two hold the upper corners and two the lower corners of the machine. When the machine is out of use, it is carried in a fibre case measuring 12 in. x 8 in. x 6 in., which also carries the harness and spare paper rolls.

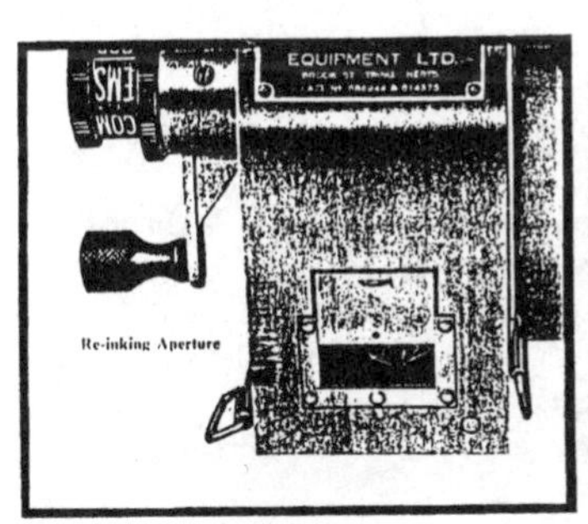

RE-INKING

ALTERING THE DATE

BIBLIOGRAPHY

Books

Aldridge, Blacker, Booth et al., *The Birth of the Routemaster*, Capital Transport, 2004
Armstrong, J., *The Bus Driver*, Educational Supply Association, 1961
Curtis, Colin, *The Routemaster Bus*, Midas, 1981
Elborough, Travis, *The Bus We Loved*, Granta, 2005
Morgan, Andrew, *Routemaster Bus Enthusiasts' Manual*, Haynes, 2011
Turner, J. F., *Timetable and Duty Schedule Compilation*, Pitman & Sons, 1946
Wagstaff, J. S., *The London Routemaster Bus*, Oakwood Press, 1975

The New Routemaster Maintenance Manual, C. & G. Walker, 1995
The Passenger Transport Year Book 1957, H. F. Maynard Ltd., 1957
The Passenger Transport Year Book 1965, Ian Allan, 1965

Newspapers & Journals

'London Transport's Routemaster: A Double-Decker Bus of Advanced Design', *Bus & Coach*, October 1954
'Routemaster Reviewed', *Buses Illustrated*, Number 21, January-March 1955
'West End Sees London's new 64-seater', *Evening News*, 31 January 1956 [LON MLD23 NPL]
'New London Bus Gives More Room', *The Star*, 31 January 1956 [LON MLD26 NPL]

TfL Archives

The following files were consulted:

(NEW)LT000515/053 Routemaster Buses
(NEW)LT000366/001 Routemaster File 1
(NEW)LT000315/9896 Bus – Routemaster
(NEW)LT000264/128 Road Services – Rolling Stock 'Routemaster' Bus
(NEW)LT000115/179 Routemaster Bus
(NEW)LT001227/214 Press Notices – London Transport Executive
(NEW)LT000366/002 Routemaster File 2
(NEW)LT000044/051 Rolling Stock – Routemaster Variations and FRM
(NEW)LT000366/004 Routemaster File 4
(NEW)LT000130/063/002 BTC: Work and Equipment Committee – Minutes
(NEW)LT000055/207 London Transport: Press Information
(NEW)LT000745/013 Trolleybus Conversion Changeover Plan – Stage 13
(NEW)LT000315/5634 The LT Routemaster Buses: A Technical Description– Text
(NEW)LT000030/044 London Transport Magazine: Volume 18
(NEW)LT0000786/045 Routemaster Buses – Instructions for Drivers and Conductors, Revised Edition (1964)
(NEW)LT001344/054 Bus RM (Routemaster)